T0161044

THE GOLDEN GOBLET
Selected Poems

Johann Wolfgang von Goethe

Translated from the German by

Zsuzsanna Ozsváth & Frederick Turner

Deep Vellum Publishing

Dallas, Texas

Deep Vellum
3000 Commerce St., Dallas, Texas 75226
deepvellum.org · @deepvellum
Deep Vellum is a 501c3
nonprofit literary arts organization founded in 2013.

ISBN: 978-1-941920-79-4 (paperback) | 978-1-941920-80-0 (ebook)
Library of Congress Control Number: 2018951693

This work is published in partnership with
the Ackerman Center for Holocaust Studies at
the University of Texas at Dallas

Cover Design by Justin Childress | justinchildress.co
Typesetting by Kirby Gann

Text set in Bembo, a typeface modeled on typefaces cut by Francesco Griffo
for Aldo Manuzio's printing of *De Aetna* in 1495 in Venice

Printed in the United States of America on acid-free paper
by McNaughton & Gunn

CONTENTS

Goethe the Revolutionary
Frederick Turner

Why read Goethe now? Or let's say: "What is wrong with us now, that we might require the help of Goethe?"

Perhaps the most dangerous feature of our times is our inability to speak to each other. That inability takes two forms, both of which have the same root. One is basically social. Everywhere we see cultural suspicions, misunderstandings, and hatreds: East and West, North and South, Muslim and Christian, rich and poor, black and white, native and immigrant, traditional and modern, young and old. The other way in which we dangerously fail to understand each other is ideological: any reader has run across the alienation between science and religion, art and science, technology and environmentalism, business and the humanities, even between disciplines like anthropology and economics, political science and sociology, philosophy and theology.

We became specialists, and, though we knew more and more about the bits of the world, we came to know less and less about the world as a whole. Is it any wonder that once we gave up any attempt to include in one view all the viewpoints and languages and jargons and dialects of the world, we could no longer agree on social, cultural, ethnic, and political issues? If there is no longer a shared language, or even an attempt at one, we stumble along blind to each other, with eyes for only what we have been trained to see; when we bump into each other, we can do nothing but fight.

Mallarmé, the great French poet and arguably one of the fathers of modernism, declared that the role of the poet is "to purify the dialect of the tribe." Sadly, we ended up purifying a thousand specializations and losing any connection between them and to the human tribe as a whole. Mallarmé was wrong. The work of the great poet is to create a common language that can connect all the thoughts and feelings of the human tribe; a supreme act of adulteration, one might say.

The old Enlightenment consensus—Reason, the Republic of Letters, the language of Jefferson, Hamilton, Franklin—did provide a shared language for a while, but it was shared only by the elites and had severe limitations, amply pointed out by the Romantics. The point of view that can transcend the shortsightedness and cruelty of the purified dialects is not just a dry Enlightenment abstraction. It is a made thing, an achievement that combines every aspect of the human being and draws on copious historical wellsprings.

Goethe is both the supreme exemplar of that perspective, that point of view, and the supreme shaper of it into an artistic whole that can serve us still. He is one of that pantheon of the great poets, the mighty adulterators of language who reset the boundaries of what humans can think or do. Their names are clichés: Homer, Vyasa, Virgil, Dante, Shakespeare, and their like. In retrospect, the great poets, adulterators all, often look very much like purifiers, so marvelous is their magic in seamlessly fusing such different fabrics and materials as they choose to weave together. But we should not be fooled. When people first heard the great poets they must have felt a shocking combination of absolute familiarity and appalling strangeness, half exhilaration and half indignation. You *can't* put words like that together! It's gauche, wicked, nastily attractive, embarrassing! Realms that we had kept comfortably apart for reasons of specialization, ethnic or religious prejudice, professional territoriality, avoidance of controversy, moral scandal, or cognitive dissonance were being embarrassingly and dangerously brought into contact. The new whole was more alarming than the sum of its parts.

Goethe's uncompromising need for a coherent and comprehensive worldview—an idea we now call "consilience"—is an ideal that is both the core of science and the most demanding goal of poetry. It virtually enforced the adoption of a view that was revolutionary, and not just for Germany. It is only now that scholars are beginning to register the shock wave that Goethe produced in the poetry of England and America.

Goethe was faced with a Europe that was already breaking up, not just on the national scale, with the collapse of the unifying ideals of the Holy Roman Empire and Christendom, but in terms of the proliferation of new sciences, disciplines, trades, philosophies, and cults. And so he set out to create a German that would do for the world what Shakespeare's English did: unify all human visions and passions into one, without denaturing any. His vision makes possible a vocabulary that can include the sciences and technical disciplines; the worldviews of cultures as diverse as those of Italy, Arabia, Persia, India, England, and China; and the whole gamut of religious passion, from defiant atheism through animism, pantheism, polytheism, and Judeo-Christian ethics to a sort of ironic philosophical monotheism of the "All-Father." His vocabulary spans also the deep history of his own language, and that of the classical languages of Europe, as well as a wide range of social class, regional dialect, and generational patois.

Goethe's color theory inspired Jan Evangelista Purkinje to commence the studies of the eye that gave birth to neuroscience.[1] Goethe is known in osteology as the discoverer of the human intermaxillary bone, in botany as the originator of the idea of the *Urpflanze*, anticipating the work of D'Arcy Thompson,[2] and more generally for his concepts of *Strebung*, *Gestalt*, and *Bildung*. Goethe grasped the vocabulary and the core ideas of a daunting range of polymaths that he knew, read, or both. They include the Humboldts, Cuvier, Young,

Torricelli, Lavoisier, Erasmus Darwin, Lamarck, Buffon, the meteorologist Luke Howard, Leibniz, Leeuwenhoek, Linnaeus, and Kant. Goethe may be the most recent plausible claimant for the title of last person to know everything.

A large part of Goethe's poetic magic is performed by his unerring and always elegantly ornamented meter and rhyme. Goethe was as much a virtuoso of meter and rhyme as Mozart was of harmony and counterpoint or Corot of tint and shade. Although he wrote in dozens of metrical forms, and in the *Odes* invents and then discards free verse a century before its time, he returns always to a perfectly rhymed alternation of feminine and masculine lines, iambic or trochaic, pentameter or tetrameter. He makes infinite variations upon that pattern, from the balladic simplicity of "Wild Rose" to the massive hexameters of "The Metamorphosis of the Plants," but it's always there. The music of that alternation is so compelling that he can fit almost any odd combination of words or worlds into it and make them feel as if they always belonged together. Part of it, I believe, is that it is a real dialectic, "masculine" and "feminine" being more than metaphorical terms for lines with heavy and light final syllables. The lines are yin and yang, thesis and antithesis, question and answer.

More specifically, Goethe exploits German's marvelous facility for inventing compound words. Goethe, like Gerard Manley Hopkins, is notorious for this, but it is not just a stylistic idiosyncrasy but an explicit sign of what Goethe is up to: making a vocabulary that will transcend the ossified categories of a culture that is falling apart.

But for all of Goethe's metrical and grammatical conjuring tricks and his stylistic control of dissent, his determination to keep all of the vocabularies of Europe (and beyond) in play must imply a larger substantive vision—a philosophy—beyond a mere eclectic ease of expression. That vision cannot but be a challenge to the whole fabric of Western thought to that point. But Goethe is no mere revolutionary: the challenge to his time is not intended to destroy it, but to heal and restore it to its full inherited grandeur, a grandeur partly achieved by the classical Greeks and during the Renaissance. If his poetry reconciles science with religion, art with ethics, political philosophy with mysticism, the humanities with the technical expertise of modern life, it is bound to offend, and here it might be illuminating to try to indicate how and where. The keys are in the multivocality of certain words—*Gestalt*, *Strebung*, and, above all, *Bildung*—and those words themselves, as he uses them, are both a threat and a promise to any established way of thought.

Gestalt, a core concept later explored brilliantly by Carl Jung, is subversive to any purely deductive reasoning: the reasoning of the Enlightenment. Its meaning proclaims that the whole is greater than the parts, that some realities are irreducible, and thus insoluble by any merely reductive scientific method. A true form or *Gestalt* is not just its elements, but the pattern and dynamic interaction of its elements. But that dynamic pattern is not ineffable and undiscoverable: the word also suggests that there might be a scientifically legitimate way of recognizing synergy and complex organization, in which levels of order can be discerned whose nature is emergent rather than given or timeless. And so the concept itself provides the opening for such ideas as evolution, ecosystem, and even the division of sciences into disciplines, where different levels of order can exist in a nested hierarchy of mathematics, physics, chemistry, biology, and social science. Emergence is today the key idea in many of the sciences (though still challenged by the reductionist-determinist establishment). The universe is not a machine whose perfectly ordered, zero-change state is disordered and decayed by time; rather, the universe *is* time, becoming, and its life and nature is change. Stable orders of various kinds, including the laws of nature, are created and maintained by that process itself. Chaos naturally gives birth to order, and order provides the tools and vocabulary for further change.

Goethe expresses this idea not only explicitly in poems like "The Metamorphosis of the Plants," "The Metamorphosis of the Animals," "Refinding," and "World Soul," but also implicitly in earlier pieces like "The Artist's Evening Song" and "On the Lake." But his sense of "organic form," as Coleridge put it in his defense of Shakespeare, is there in every one of his poems, in their integrity and synergetic self-reference. Goethe ruefully points out how hard this is to achieve in his sonnet on the sonnet form:

The Sonnet

To practice a revived artistic kind
Is an expected, holy obligation:
You too may follow the prescribed dictation,
As step by step it regulates your mind.
For what you loved was how the form confined
In limits the wild spirits' agitation;
However violent their inclination,
The work would find its shaped and proper end.
So I'd in artful sonnets like to fettle
With rhyme and measure eloquent and limber
Whatever my emotion gave to do;
For this, though, I can't comfortably settle,
Loving to hew things from a single timber,
And otherwise would sometimes have to glue.

Notice how, in his artistic mastery, he has perfectly fitted his apology for his metrical imperfections into the strict Petrarchan metrical form. (It was I, the translator, who had to "glue" with the half-rhyme.)

As with *Gestalt*, the inscape[3] and subtle internal synergy of natural beings and genuine human creations, the idea of *Strebung*—striving, inclination, tendency, proclivity, effort—undermines older top-down conceptions of nature. Natural beings, animate and perhaps even inanimate, contain strivings, affinities, a rage for order, an order that rages. Why should desire, so pervasive among humans and animals, have been suddenly injected into an indifferent universe? Why shouldn't its more primitive versions have existed always already in matter, energy, and light, as he insists in "World Soul" and "Ur-Words: Orphic"? What makes desire a less worthy candidate for cosmic primacy than time and space? Desire is active: Faust's reinterpretation of the beginning of the Gospel of John is: "In the beginning was the act." In "The Metamorphosis of the Plants," he speeds up the emergence of the leaves and flowers to show how urgently, how pruriently, the plant desires its last ejaculation of blossom. Anyone who has cruelly pinched off the flowers of a basil plant, and who has seen in the next few hours how quickly and with what frustration it throws out new leaves to muster the energy for sexual replacements, will know what he means.

God, for Goethe, is not the external puppet master pulling the strings of natural action: God is the internal urge of the action itself, its joy in making, its impatience and seeking. "Striving" in both German and English is related to strife; to strive is to compete, even to fight, but with the specific sense of a higher goal that transcends the fight itself. Goethe's work (especially considering the bloody Napoleonic times in which he lived) is remarkably free of fights, battles, and violence; like Darwin, he sees that the great competition is over not who is going to be the best destroyer, but who is going to be the most successful creator, cooperator, lover, contributor, who will best shape an ecosystem that will ensure survival. For Goethe, as for Teilhard de Chardin (the great French evolutionist and theologian) *le milieu divin*, the divine environment, is not stasis but becoming; what is eternal is not a fixed form but an unresting drive toward form, toward forms more beautiful, synergetic, and profound in meaning.

In insisting on the validity of striving, Goethe is questioning other more comfortable styles of life. *Strebung* can be used socially as a term of contempt. The bourgeois striver is despised by the aristocrat, who never needs to break a sweat and needs no ambition. The aspiring artist is a figure of pity. The anxious and curious philosophical seeker is looked down on by the man of sure faith. The guilty sinner, still striving for redemption, who has at least had the courage to break the rules, is damned by the complacent moralist, who has not had the inner fire and juice to be tempted. Goethe sees self-improvement, ambition, effort, skeptical curiosity, emulation, and the battle against failure as the supreme virtues; Faust is redeemed by them.

Bildung is the combination of *Strebung* and *Gestalt* within a developing human personality: the striving is toward form; the form is the product of past striving and the ground of further striving. In nature, the general form of that striving is expressed in the German word *Entwicklung*, dear to Goethe, usually translated today as "evolution." We are now familiar with the strange attractors of nonlinear dynamical systems and chaotic self-organization, with those amazing foliate forms that we see in the Mandelbrot set and other fractal visualizations. We are the new Platonists, able now to trace and mathematically model with some accuracy the ideal forms of nature, though we find those forms not in the timelessness of Plato's geometrical idealizations and generalizations, not in their stillness, but in the heart of motion and time. But Goethe in many ways got there before us: his *Urpflanze*, his archetypal leaf, is none other than a strange attractor, the always-not-quite-achieved goal of a nonlinear dynamical system, unmistakable in its style but highly variable and differentiated in its physical instances. And the *Entwicklung* of a human person is his *Bildung*.

Goethe's conception of evolution was much like that of his contemporary Jean-Baptiste de Lamarck (1744–1829), in that it included the idea of "soft inheritance," that is, the biological inheritance of individually acquired characteristics. This idea was later roundly rejected by the Darwinians, who maintained that the only way an individual could contribute to its species' evolution was by either giving birth to offspring or dying without them and not passing on its inheritance. Differential rates of survival over many generations would do the heavy lifting of sorting out beneficial survival traits from deleterious ones.

But Goethe and Lamarck (and Schelling, Goethe's protégé, who had similar views) may have been closer to the truth than evolutionists have believed until the last couple of decades. It now appears that genes can be turned on or off through mechanisms like methylation or phosphorylation, and that the patterns of "off" and "on" genes are controlled by regulatory genes or even by mysterious processes in the nongenetic bulk of the DNA sequence. Those control and regulatory systems are themselves highly sensitive to both the experiences and the actions of the individual to which they belong, and thus the actions and experiences of an organism can change the organism itself. How you live your life—what choices you make, what training or education you take on, what places and states you explore—can actually change the action of your genes in generating your body and mind, and thus transform you even if your basic complement of genes does not change at all. You can play the genetic cards you've been given in the order and combinations you choose, and you don't have to play all the cards in your hand.

The big point is that such self-transformation, the pattern of genes that are turned on or off, is inheritable. We can to a limited extent pass down our experience *biologically* to our offspring, and they to theirs. The genes do not change, but their expression can, quite decisively. This means that the *Strebung* of one generation, in enduring or acting, doing or suffering, is passed on to the future; that inheritance might in turn very strongly affect how good an individual's chances of having or not having offspring would be. Freedom—literal self-determination—now becomes an essential part of the work of species-making and species survival. The individual is not a mere pawn or puppet, but a player. Such a process, multiplied across a whole gene pool, can massively accelerate the rate by which differential survival can alter the frequency of the genes and thus the species itself.

There is an important literary implication in Goethe's belief that we are not just the passive products of our biological heritage, but active self-determining participants in the advance of our species. If, as seems likely, scientists of our own time are now endorsing the truth of this observation, perhaps it behooves us to consider whether Goethe's view of the human condition may be more appropriate than those of the many writers, modern and postmodern, who have assumed that we are basically the puppets of our genetic inheritance and passive victims of history. Our Strebung can create our *Gestalt*, and the process can result in *Bildung*. The future is in our hands, not fate's or chance's—or in those of our "race."

For Goethe culture is nature by other means, second nature, and nature is the culture of the beings that preceded us and exist around us. Poetry is fast evolution; evolution is slow poetry. Nature is not, so to speak, on a single track into the future, and neither are we. We certainly are pressed by our past inheritance, driven by urges and desires, but how we choose and combine them determines not only our immediate actions in the moment but also what kind of being we will be in the future. Time is branchy, and we can take at any moment one branch rather than another. An act or deed—in German, *Tat*—is not just an event or a result, but a cause in itself. "Im Anfang war die Tat."[4] And this freedom to choose is not a strange unnatural or supernatural supervention into a world that is otherwise a deterministic machine (as existentialists of various stripes have maintained) but a property of nature itself in its own branching and self-tracing path. Human intention is just as determinative of the world as are physical laws; the physical laws may have emerged earlier in the generation of the world, but that causative latecomer, human intention, can itself move mountains or, like Faust's great sea walls, hold back the ocean itself by harnessing those very laws.

If we are free in this sense of self-determining, and if, as Goethe strongly feels, that free spontaneity is the most important part of a human being, then the base of religious morality must be radically shifted. Not that morality should be overthrown, but rather it must be made to fit a new foundation: not obedience but freedom. There is still sin, but the sin is not to transgress but to imprison. The new consilience he demands, in which moral rules cannot be allowed to remain separate from biological and physical science and the new philosophy of a dynamic world that is implied by it, requires a critique of traditional sexual morality. And it is, of course, sex where we see best the wild riskiness and driving energy of physical life in its free creative and generative adventure, sex that is the battleground where Goethe meets the old prescriptions and proscriptions. His poem "The Bride of Corinth" is a searing indictment of sexual repression. It ruthlessly diagnoses the psychological sickness that leads a parent to sacrifice her own child to a cold creed that is a comfort to the weak. Both Freud and Nietzsche surely paid attention.

Goethe's poetic vocation of consilience thus led him to wrestle with the God of his times. Though the wrestling match begins with his early adventures in the world of sexual love, so triumphantly celebrated in such poems as "Maying," "Welcome and Farewell," and "Wild Rose," its defiance of religious authority is only implicit there and has not yet spread to other areas of contention. Why, Goethe begins to ask, does there have to be only one divine economy? Struck by the beauty of the Greco-Roman pantheon and the humaneness of a world where different kinds of fate can be chosen according to the god to whom one makes sacrifice, he begins to challenge the hegemony of monotheism. His poem "Take This to Heart" epitomizes this strategy.

Still, and always, Goethe keeps the notion of the "All-Father," but the conception is variously separated from the abstract infinite moralistic punisher of standard eighteenth-century religion. The Father becomes one of many gods, he is Romanized or Hellenized or Islamized, he has a thousand names, and most of all he becomes the heart and soul of natural forces, not their enemy and censor. Like Blake and Nietzsche, Goethe transvalues divinity; Urizen, "Your Reason," is deposed and replaced by Los, the spirit of energy and imagination who is always implicit in the Fall and the loss of paradise—a paradise to be replaced by a creative process, by *Bildung*.

What comes next is Goethe's denial and refutation of theodicy, the justification of suffering in the divine economy. He especially objects to suffering as a divinely just punishment for disobedience. Suffering, rather, is the accompaniment of aspiration to godhead. And Goethe presents his All-Father with a choice: *be* our striving, our power against fate, our friend and co-conspirator in the siege of Heaven, or be the cold and demanding authority figure and take the risk of being overthrown or at least exposed as morally inferior to Your creations. Perhaps Goethe on balance gives God the benefit of the doubt and takes Him on as a friend and potential equal, especially in the *West-East Divan* poems. But this must mean that Mephistopheles is His accomplice, His double agent.

When the traditional theological language is put under such radical stresses and transformations and becomes a play space for speculation rather than a secure deposit of faith, the language itself becomes complex and ironized. In "Divinity," the balance is especially complex and rich:

> But Man alone
> May do the impossible:
> He makes distinctions,
> Chooses, judges;
> He can to the moment
> Grant permanence.
>
> He alone may
> Reward the good,
> Punish the evil,
> Heal and save
> All that's in error,
> Use and connect.
>
> And so we honor
> Those the undying ones
> As if they were human
> Acting in great things
> As the best man in small things
> Does, or desires to do.
>
> Noble humanity,
> Be good and merciful!
> Create untiringly
> The useful, the righteous,
> Be for us an image
> Of those guessed beings!

Goethe seems to have solved at least part of his problems with religion by radically compounding it with science. Natural evolution is not for him a refutation of divine creation but its explication and concrete enactment. Language in the absence of a timeless, supernatural, and infinite God need not fall apart (as I believe the Deconstructionists implied); rather, it regains a power it lost when God was translated out of nature. Language becomes one with the creative force of evolution, which continues in human history, in human creativity, and—especially—in poetry. Science's need to change the meanings of words and make up new words led the way. In Goethe's lifetime, over thirty new elements were discovered, isolated, and named. Goethe gloried in the newly emerging vocabularies of botany, anatomy, and climatology, as we may see in such works as "The Metamorphosis of the Plants" and "In Honor of Luke Howard." Adam's task of naming is also God's.

It is religious miracle that Goethe objects to, not simply on Spinoza's ground that its definition is self-contradictory, but because he finds nature itself so miraculous that any such intervention into it would be crass and despicable, a lie, a cheat. What is taken to be the supernatural is in his view a vulgar escape hatch from reality; for him, the true supernatural is an inherent element in all process and becoming, in time itself. Goethe's many demons and spirits and gods and naiads are all, like those of the Greeks and Romans, part of Nature itself. Nature "supernatures" itself anyway, in every moment, by generating out of all the possible futures the one it chooses, creating new reality all the time. Blinded by custom, we cannot be properly amazed, and we look elsewhere for a tawdry amazement. For Goethe, Nature is all the revelation we need; the scriptures of the religions can be beautiful poetry, to be freely retranslated, as Faust does with the Book of John, according to our growing wisdom. But they are not literal truth, and their fictive miracles are symbols of mysterious natural processes.

Goethe is tactful, however, and respects the feelings of believers. Faust's conversation with Gretchen, with its definitely comic overtones, is a good example of Goethe's own gentle quizzing of the faithful:

MARGARETE:
. . . Do you believe in God?

FAUST: Love, who can say
"Yes, I believe in God"?
Ask the priest and wise man, and what they
Will answer sounds like mockery
Of her who asks the question.

MARGARETE:
                                   So you don't believe?

FAUST:
Oh, sweet-faced innocent, don't misconceive!
Who can name Him,
Who can claim Him,
Saying "I believe"?
Who presume
To say "I don't believe"?
The all-containing,
All-sustaining,
Does He not embrace, sustain
You, and myself, and Him?
Above, does not the sky arch high,
Below, the firm earth steadfast lie?
Do not the friendly stars eternal rise,
Do we not see each other, eyes in eyes?
And do not all things strive
Toward your head and heart,
And do not all things weave

Themselves with everlasting secrecy,
Seen thus unseen, into your closest intimacy?
     Fill up your heart with this,
And when your feelings overflow with bliss
Name it as you wish by any name whatever!
Luck, call it! Heart! Love! God!
I have no name to call it!
Feeling is all—
A name is but sound and smoke,
Clouding the glow of heaven.

MARGARETE:
This is all well and good.
It's what the priest says, more or less,
Except the words are rather different.

For all Goethe's daring intellectual adventures—with their continuing reverberations into the present—his ideas are not dry logical stalks but engorged growing shoots, bursting into flower. He is as passionate a poet as he is a philosophical or scientific one. For him, moral freedom is not a negative affair of rational choice and tolerance and unamazement but a plunge into a state of huge moral and existential risk, an adventure of the spirit.

So the comprehensiveness, the *adulteratedness*, of Goethe's poetic vocabulary extends to that much more ancient, contextual, action-oriented, profound, and survival-based form of thinking that we call emotion. Rhetoric is the discipline of putting that rich form of thinking into words. Goethe shows how persuasion can happen when poetry extends its vocabulary to include all the points of view of the language community, and we are enabled to speak to each other's whole being—hearts, minds, bodies, and all.

ENDNOTES

1. See *Purkinje's Vision: The Dawning of Neuroscience* by Nicholas J. Wade and Josef Brožek in collaboration with Jiří Hoskovec (Mahwah, NJ: Lawrence Erlbaum Associates, 2001), 1–2 and *passim*.

2. See *Morphogenesis: Origins of Patterns and Shapes*, eds. Paul Bourgine and Annick Lesne (New York: Springer, 2011), 295.

3. Gerard Manley Hopkins's term for the inner form and energy of a natural entity.

4. "In the beginning was the act." Faust translating the Book of John.

Biography as Poetry, Poetry as Biography
Zsuzsanna Ozsváth

> Goethe's lyrics constitute the most splendid treasure of
> all German poetry. There may be German-language
> authors whose poetic work has larger scope, but none
> has produced as much poetry that remains vivid even
> now or that is as magnificent as on the first day; and none
> has poems that are more tender and ingenious, more
> colorfully dazzling and versatile, more contemplative and
> vivacious than his.[1]

Our translations of Goethe's poetry concentrate on a rela-
tively small portion of his lyrical achievement—especially if
we include works such as *Faust* (1771–1832) and *Iphigenia
in Tauris* (1785) as part of his poetic oeuvre. Yet we believe
that our selection provides a starting point, since it contains
a significant number of the author's major poems, represent-
ing his most important artistic phases of creative expression
and powerful imagination. In addition, it attempts to capture
both the musical structure and the vitality of the originals.

Growing up in Frankfurt: 1749–1765
Born on August 28, 1749, in Frankfurt am Main, Johann
Wolfgang von Goethe was the son of enlightened, well-ed-
ucated, prosperous parents who were dedicated to their chil-
dren and raised them in a highly intellectual, artistic milieu.
Goethe was just a boy when he started to read and write
poetry, and he was enchanted by the lyrics, stories, and plays
to which he was exposed. In his early teens, he saw every
new performance at the Frankfurt Theater and composed
poetry, using new metaphors, ideas, and images. By the time

he was sixteen and enrolled as a student at the University of Leipzig, he was well-known among his peers, who considered him an authority in the field of poetry.

Student Life in Leipzig: 1765–68

At first, Goethe looked forward to enrolling at the University of Göttingen: he hoped to study classical philology. But he eventually accepted his father's wish that he become a lawyer and enrolled in law school at Leipzig University. Yet while taking classes in his major, the poet did not give up his interests in art and literature. In fact, his desire to become an active member of the literary community intensified. He continued to follow his childhood passion, remaining fascinated by the world of the theater and seeing every new play performed in town. In addition, he not only regularly attended lectures on the development of various aesthetic approaches to literature, but he was also eager to hear and read about the discussions on art and poetry going on among the famous German writers and artists of the time. At this point in his life, he knew that he wanted nothing as much as to create and think, argue, and write about new art and literature. His interest created serious concerns in his family and intensified the tension between him and his father. He tried to suppress his feelings as much as he could—to no avail. The conflict between father and son deepened.

Back in Frankfurt: 1768–1770

After three years studying law in Leipzig, Goethe fell ill. He left his studies and returned to his parents' home, where he spent eighteen months recuperating.[2] During this time, he read widely and became familiar with some of the leading intellectual and religious movements of the time—among them Pietism, a reform movement in German Lutheranism. The young poet learned about this mystical, devotional movement, emphasizing the subjective aspects of faith, striving to revive piety over religion, orthodoxy, and ritual. Not quite twenty years old, Goethe was at first truly exalted: he turned his interest toward several mystical philosophers, whose beliefs and ideas influenced his thinking. It was obviously part of Goethe's "deep search for faith" that inspired him to begin reading about hermeticism, alchemy, and the history of the heretics. But after a while, Goethe turned away from both mysticism and Pietism alike. Most critics—among them the editors of *Faust*—believe the reason for this change lay in Goethe's rejection of the concept of the sinfulness of human nature. They claim that: "It must have been [the Pietists'] fundamental assumption, which Goethe couldn't share, that made him turn his back on the movement altogether."[3]

Law School in Strasbourg: 1770–71

After much soul-searching, Goethe enrolled at Strasbourg Law School. In addition, he found intense literary and cultural stimulation in this town, coming from several major writers and scholars of the period—among them Johann Gottfried Herder, a highly influential figure in German intellectual circles of the early 1770s. Besides Homer, Pindar, and Shakespeare, Herder studied the Bible and embraced German national history. These interests influenced Goethe's life and his emotional, intellectual, and aesthetic development. Also, the poet recognized the importance of Herder's call for the resurrection of the German national past; much of Goethe's early poetry illustrates this development.

Using the native tradition of the folk song as a basic approach for one of Goethe's best-known early lyrics, the poem "Wild Rose" (1770) captures the tragic outcome of true passion suffered by a young girl, whose life is destroyed by a boy who seduces and leaves her:

> Once a boy a wild rose spied,
> Rosebud in the heather;

Young and fresh as morningtide,
Ran to see, all eager-eyed,
Joyful, gazing thither.
Rosebud, rosebud, rosebud red,
Rosebud in the heather.

Then the boy said: I'll pick you,
Rosebud in the heather!
Rosebud answered: I'll prick you,
I'll not be forgot by you:
I'll not bear it either.
Rosebud, rosebud, rosebud red,
Rosebud in the heather.

And the rude lad plucked her then,
Rosebud from the heather;
Rosebud pricked him, but in vain
Was for her all grief and pain,
She must ache forever.
Rosebud, rosebud, rosebud red,
Rosebud in the heather.[4]

It is the tonality of traditional German verse that reso-
nates in this poem, creating its compositional wholeness. Its
rhymes and rhythms come from a distant past, revived by
Goethe's new aesthetic decision: to return to the approach,
feelings, and mode of the ancient German folk song by
using its form and poetic expression. Influenced by Herder,
the poet decided to turn against the rococo style and the sti-
fling artistic etiquette of his time, together with the neoclas-
sical regulations of French verse-making, all of which had
dominated German culture for many years.

One of the first examples of Goethe's decision on the
need to "return to the past" was formulated in his famous
essay, "On German Architecture."[5] In it, the poet calls for

a new vision and a new approach to art. Extolling the aesthetic power of the cathedral in Strasbourg, he describes the importance of recreating "the ancient German approach to architecture." In addition, he emphasizes the need to bring back the art of the past and enlarges his own poetic vision and lyrical expression by reading Shakespeare, Pindar, and Homer.

Along with the cultural, aesthetic, and linguistic epiphany Goethe underwent in Strasbourg, he also experienced a major love affair. He met Friederike Brion, the daughter of a pastor in the nearby village of Sesenheim. He wrote to her several erotic love poems, whose lasting impact is still present in twentieth- and twenty-first-century German poetry.[7] We have translated "Welcome and Farewell" (1770):

> But ah, the sun, already rising,
> Tightened the farewell in my heart:
> What joy was in your kiss, amazing!
> What pain was in your eyes, what smart!
> I left, you stood there earthward gazing,
> Then stole a moist glance after me;
> But to be loved, what joy past praising,
> And—Gods!—to love, what ecstasy![7]

The relationship between Friederike and the young poet was never consummated, however, and in August 1771, the twenty-two-year-old Goethe withdrew from the young girl—as he would withdraw from almost all of his intensely passionate love affairs. Some of his biographers believe that he cut off his involvements because he feared they would result in stifled feelings or, even worse, he would be "permanently caught" by one of his lovers. Whatever the reason, the relationship with Friederike, as well as the couple's separation, had a significant impact on Goethe's life and a lasting influence on German poetry. Several of the poems published in the *Sesenheim Songs* bear witness to the extraordinary depth of this intense yet painful experience of love and to the poet's expression of passionate emotion in poetry.

Goethe's Rising Fame: Frankfurt—Wetzlar—Frankfurt, 1771–74

In the fall of 1771, after receiving his degree, Goethe moved back to Frankfurt and started a private practice. In May 1772, he moved to Wetzlar, where he worked as a lawyer for five months. During this period he composed some of his famous hymns, which changed the direction of German literature. Among them, "Wanderer's Storm Song" created a new language for the *Sturm und Drang* (Storm and Stress) movement, a language that contains motifs from the ancient Greek myths and the Bible. This poem also reflects Goethe's belief in the divine power of the artist:

> Not rain, nor storm,
> Can shake his heart
> Whom you have not forsaken, Genius.
> Against the hailstorm,
> Against the cloud-wrack
> He whom you have not deserted
> Will be singing
> Like the lark, Genius,
> O you on high![8]

Besides new ideas that placed the artist-poet next to the gods, Goethe was inspired by both Shakespeare's dramatic approach to literature and Herder's urgings to discover national history in culture. At this point of his life, he felt the need to write about the German past. Reading the biography of a robber baron, a known character during the German Peasants' War (1524–25), he decided to use that story for his major drama, *Götz of Berlichingen* (1773–74), a play that achieved immediate national fame. At this point, most German writers and poets regarded Goethe as the greatest literary genius of the period and a major figure in the creation of the new literary movement. This movement hailed stormy passions and highly emotional relationships as the foremost experiences of human life and was popular among most young German poets of the time. It emphasized intense feelings and irrationalism, while stressing the human need for emotional turbulence, passion, and subjectivity. Its followers viewed inner struggles, depth of feeling, individualism, and potential for passionate love as the highest, most tragic and chaotic, and, at the same time, the most vital driving forces of human experience, anticipating Freud's observations of the id by more than a hundred years.

In 1774, two years after *Götz*, twenty-five-year-old Goethe published his epistolary novel *The Sorrows of Young Werther*, yet another tale born out of the *Sturm und Drang* movement.[9] The book revolves around a young man, Werther, who suffers passionate yet unfulfilled love for a young girl who marries another. Goethe wrote this novel at a time when he, like his protagonist, was feeling the pain of rejected love. In real life, he had fallen in love with a young girl, Charlotte Buff, who was already engaged to (and then married) Goethe's friend Johann Kestner. The novel ends with Werther's suicide. It reflects Goethe's own pain in his unrequited love for Charlotte and his identification with his young acquaintance Karl Jerusalem, who committed suicide after a tragic love affair. At this point, there was no longer any question about which profession the poet should choose. *Werther* made him world-famous.

Clearly, Goethe's life experience affected his poetry. He wanted to be free, but whenever he extricated himself from a relationship, he would endure unbearable suffering at the loss of the beloved. Such emotions are reflected not only in the story of *Werther*, but also in the tales of several other love affairs appearing in the poet's oeuvre. In fact, as Denis de Rougemont has described in his book *Love in the Western World*, the close relationship between passion and death is a recurring theme underlying our culture.[10] In this way, *Werther* recalls the tales of Lancelot and Guinevere, Orpheus and Eurydice, Tristan and Isolde, Romeo and Juliet, and other love affairs that play a major role in Western culture, portraying passion as a dangerous drive that promises happiness but brings suffering and death. Goethe also used this motif in his play *Egmont*. Here Klärchen speaks about her love in some of the most moving lines in world literature:

> Joyful
> And woeful
> And brooding in vain;
> Longing
> And fearing,
> Suspended in pain;
> Sky-high elated
> And dying with rue,
> Happy alone
> Is the soul that loves true.[11]

Publishing *Werther*, Goethe stayed in Frankfurt for one more year. In 1774, he composed many new poems, among them his famous hymns. Several of these appear in this volume: "Ganymede," "Prometheus," "Cousin Kronos," and others, including another famous poem, "The King in Thule," written in the style of a folk song. He also finished his dramas *Götz*, *Clavigo*, and *Stella*, and he wrote a number of short dramatic scenes and some of the major segments of *Faust*.

In 1775, near end of his stay in Frankfurt and while continuing to write, the poet fell in love again. This time, he became engaged to Anna Elisabeth "Lili" Schönemann, a beautiful young woman from an influential family. But just before he left for Weimar, Goethe broke off the engagement: the relationship between him and the young girl ended abruptly.[12]

Goethe in Weimar: 1775–1786

The year 1775 was of great significance for Goethe. At the invitation of the eighteen-year-old duke Karl August, ruler of the small duchy of Weimar, the poet was appointed to a ministerial position within a few months of his arrival. Suddenly, he had a wide range of major administrative obligations, including organizing the economic development of the duchy. He served as a member of the duke's privy council and became the chief administrator of its army, taking on the service of both the war commission and the highway commission. He also oversaw the production of the duchy's mines, fields, and forests. While studying the region's botanical, zoological, and geological growth, the poet was intellectually and artistically inspired, developing new ideas and discovering new aspects of the natural world.

Walking the roads of the region and studying the countryside, he also composed poetry and some of the major scenes of his play *Iphigenia in Tauris*. We have translated two of his major lyrical compositions, revealing his reaction to natural changes and the underlying unifying principles of biological processes as expressed in the terms of his new poetic vision ("Metamorphosis of the Plants" and "Metamorphosis of the Animals"). As a reward for his dedication to the development of the duchy, the duke ennobled Goethe in 1782.

While attentive to the complexity of plants, their natural growth, and their development, Goethe hoped to understand the nature of spiritual change in human culture as well, studying languages and their expression, especially in poetry. He learned English, French, Hebrew, Arabic, Chinese, and other languages to become better acquainted with the cultures of various countries. And, as he walked among the villages, he would often stop on his way and talk to the peasants working in the fields, learning from them some of the ancient German folk songs. Among many other poems, his breathtaking "Elf-King" (*Erlkönig*), set to music by Schubert, shows the ways in which he mastered the connection between the music of the words and the events the text projects. The wild riding of the father with his sick son emphasizes the parent's desperate fight for the child's life against the threat of death, manifested in the poem's breathless flow; meanwhile, the words themselves carry the fear of the trembling father, the anxiety of the little boy, and the seductive power of the ghost, with their words underscoring the rhythm of the galloping horse. Four voices resound at times; at others, there are two or three:

> Who rides so late through wind and night?
> A father with his child so white.
> He holds the boy within his arm,
> Hugging him fast to keep him warm . . .
>
> "My son, why hide your face in fear?"
> "D'you see the Elf-King, Father dear,
> The Elven-King with cape and crown?"
> "My son, 'tis fog upon the down." . . .
>
> "Sweet child, come with me now away;
> Such lovely games we two will play,
> Such lovely flowers upon the strand,
> And golden robes from my mother's hand."

The more the Elf-King talks to the child, the more frightening the run of the horse, the heavier the breathing of the father, and the more terrifying the threat against the boy, who dies at the end:

The father in horror rides like the gale
In his arms the moaning child so pale,
He comes to the house in toil and dread:
But in his arms the child was dead.[13]

Throughout the centuries, many of the great compos-
ers (Mozart, Beethoven, Schubert, Schumann, Brahms,
Mendelssohn, Berlioz, Mahler, and others) have set Goethe's
poetry to music. Several of these poems appear in our trans-
lations, and we have tried to recreate in English the music
of the original.

Goethe's musical approach is capable of integrating our
auditory perception with our visual experience. In *Wilhelm
Meister* (1796), he describes Italy as a place where:

> . . . lemon blossoms blow,
> Where in dark leaves the orange goldfruit glow,
> Where the mild wind wafts from the azure sky,
> The myrtle's still, the bay leaf shines on high—[14]

Soon after his arrival at the court of Weimar in 1775,
Goethe fell in love with Charlotte von Stein, who had been
married for many years. Seven years older than the poet, she
had already given birth to seven children. Still, he adored
her. Thus began an all-consuming love affair based on res-
ignation and self-sacrifice rather than urgent desire, flaming
emotion, and happy expectation. He claimed that he loved
her soul, while she calmed his passion in ways that charac-
terize the relationship between sister and brother, husband
and wife. He expressed this perception in the poem, "To
Charlotte von Stein"—which, too, may be found among
our translations:

> Say, what fate is even now preparing,
> Say, how first it bound us, life to life?

In some former age that we were sharing,
You were my sister, or my own true wife![15]

Yet with all the success in work, the poet's emotional life did not significantly improve. The years passed, and despite the depth of his frustrated passion for Charlotte—or perhaps because of it—and despite his friendship with the duke and his influence at court, Goethe grew tired of Weimar. Having served for ten years in the government of the duchy, he needed to escape. As Nicholas Boyle observes, "after 10 years in Weimar, [Goethe] was intellectually and emotionally on the verge of bankruptcy."[16] The poet left town in a hurry.

The Italian Journey: 1786–88
Leaving Weimar in 1786, Goethe spent almost two years in Italy, the country he loved and had yearned for all his life. The Italian trip brought him tremendous professional and emotional fulfillment. He decided to change his style in art, using a new approach based on the classical art of ancient Greece and Rome. After returning to Weimar in 1888, he followed up on his decision to reconceive, reinvent, and recreate the Italian Renaissance in Germany.

This new, radical idea affected another poet and playwright of the time, Friedrich Schiller. The two men created a new style in art and literature: German neoclassicism.

Goethe also found great emotional fulfillment and happiness in Italy. It is not clear whether he met an otherwise unnamed woman who appears as "Faustine" in *The Roman Elegies* (1788–1790, first entitled *Erotica Romana*), a collection of twenty-four poems, or whether this woman was actually someone else. All we know from this series of erotic poems is that Goethe had a passionate sexual relationship with a young woman in Italy and that he wrote about and celebrated this experience in his poetry. As he declares in the "Fifth Elegy":

She being conquered by sleep, I lie there envouled
    with thoughts;
Often within her arms, I've written the poem already,
Counted with fingering hand along the line of her
    spine
Softly the measured hexameter. She breathes in
    lovely slumber,
Breath that glowingly penetrates into the depth of
    my breast.
Amor trims the lamp and thinks of the many ages,
Musing upon the triumvirs, they whose will he once
    served.[17]

Goethe's Return to Weimar: 1788–1832

In 1788, the poet went back to Weimar. Shocking the town, he lived openly with a young woman, Christiane Vulpius, until they married in 1806. The couple had several children, of whom just one, August, survived. But he, too, died young, two years before Goethe.

After he resettled in Weimar, significant changes took place in Goethe's life. He freed himself from the official duties that had previously stifled him both emotionally and artistically. In 1789, he became the director of the recently founded Weimar Court Theatre, staging a number of new productions as well as creating a platform for his own classical dramas and those of Schiller. At this point in their careers, both poets had arrived at the height of the artistic style they called "Classicism," turning decisively against the two major avant-garde literary movements of their time, *Sturm und Drang* and Romanticism—both of which they had helped to invent and develop. Soon after Goethe resettled in Weimar, he rewrote much of his unfinished work, completing both *Egmont* (1788) and *Tasso* (1790), reviving *Werther*, and publishing *The Roman Elegies* (1795).

In addition to his dedication to classical art and literature, the poet was deeply interested in some of the major aspects of science. He collected and studied plants, minerals, and animal specimens. He even discovered the intermaxillary bone in the human jaw (although not the first to note it, he made this discovery independently). And while his *Theory of Colors* has not been validated by the science of optical physics, his description of color has been recognized by neurobiologists as having inspired the origins of the neuroscience of vision.[18]

With many changes in style and approach over the years, Goethe wrote love poems throughout his life. In the period 1814–15, he became fascinated with Middle Eastern poetry, starting work on a series of poems entitled *The West-East Divan*. We have translated eight poems from this series. They originate from a collection of lyrics inspired by Goethe's love affair with Marianne Willemer, a woman who had collaborated with him on this project and who had probably composed several of its major pieces.

In his seventies, Goethe fell in love with Ulrike von Levetzow, to whom he wrote some of the most beautiful love poems in all world literature—many of which anticipate "modernist" poetry. Yet three summers after the affair started, the pair separated. Goethe was heartbroken. His response to this tragic breakup was the "Marienbad Elegy," particularly, the second part of the "Trilogy of Passion," which appears in this volume of our translations. Its lyrics are described by John R. Williams as "the most unequivocally and viscerally tragic lyrical expression of [Goethe's] poetic oeuvre."[19]

Goethe wrote about art and nature as well as about love and the artistic imagination, and he continued examining these themes until the end of his life. He finished the edition of his first *Collected Works* in 1787–1790; *Egmont* and *Iphigenia* in 1787–89; *Torquato Tasso* and *The Roman Elegies* in 1790; he wrote *Xenien* with Schiller in 1795; and published both *Wilhelm Meister's Apprenticeship* and *Hermann and Dorothea* in 1796. Among some of his major poems and many other pieces, he completed *Faust Part I* in 1806 and finished the novel *Elective Affinities* in 1809; he wrote the *Theory of Colors* in 1800–1810 and *The West-East Divan* in 1814–19. In addition, he finished *Poetry and Truth*, his discussions about his life and work, in 1812, and, in 1821, *Wilhelm Meister's Journey*. Finally, in 1831, he concluded *Faust Part II*, which was published posthumously in 1832.

Losing Christiane in 1816, Goethe lived to see the birth of three of his grandchildren, and then, tragically, the death of his only surviving son, August, in 1830. Admired and loved by his contemporaries, the poet stayed in Weimar for the rest of his life. He died on March 22, 1832, and was buried next to Schiller in the Vault of the Princes (*Fürstengruft*).

The poems we have chosen to translate play a major role not only in Goethe's oeuvre, but also in the development of modern German lyrical language. Starting with his early work, we have translated poems from the various periods of Goethe's lyrical creation. All of them demonstrate the author's freedom of expression, imagination, and unique musical achievement. We have also attempted to echo their composer's sensuous, incantatory, and always powerfully emotional voice.

To introduce Goethe's work in chronological order is a difficult enterprise. Because he sometimes arranged his collections according to theme, form, and genre, it is not always possible to determine a poem's date of composition. In addition, he would sometimes substantially change the texts of his lyrics. Still, following the order of the publication of his work, we have tried as much as possible to group the poems chronologically. Our goal has been to translate Goethe's poetry into English, approximating its musical, rhythmical, and visual achievement, and opening the door to this new world of treasures for English-speaking readers.

ENDNOTES

1. *Herrlich wie am ersten Tag: 125 Gedichte und ihre Interpretationen*, ed. Marcel Reich-Ranicki (Frankfurt am Main und Leipzig: Insel, 2009), 19. (My translation.)

2. Nicholas Boyle, *Goethe: The Poet and the Age: Volume I: The Poetry of Desire (1749–1790)* (Oxford: Oxford University Press, 1991), 70–73. According to Boyle, Goethe suffered a serious hemorrhage and experienced one relapse after another.

3. Johann Wolfgang von Goethe, *Faust*, ed. R-M. S. Heffner, Helmut Rehder, and W.F. Twaddell (Madison: The University of Wisconsin Press, 1975), vol. 1, 105.

4. Johann Wolfgang von Goethe, "Heidenröslein," in *Gedichte: 1756–1799*, ed. Karl Eibl (Frankfurt am Main: Deutscher Klassiker Verlag, 1998), 278.

5. Johann Wolfgang von Goethe, "Von deutscher Baukunst," in *Werke*, ed. Erich Trunz, Hans Joachim Schrimpf, and Herbert von Einem (Hamburg: Hamburger Ausgabe, 1960), vol. 12, 7–15.

6. We have translated three poems from the time of the poet's relationship with Friederike: "Welcome and Farewell," "Maying," and "Wild Rose."

7. "Willkommen und Abschied," in *Gedichte*, 283.

8. "Wanderers Sturmlied," in *Gedichte*, 195–98.

9. Johann Wolfgang von Goethe, *Die Leiden des Jungen Werthers*, in *Gedenkausgabe der Werke, Briefe, und Gespräche*, ed. Ernst Beutler (Zurich: Artemis Verlag, 1948), vol. 4.

10. Denis de Rougemont, *Love in the Western World*, trans. Montgomery Belgion (Princeton: Princeton University Press, 1983).

11. Johann Wolfgang von Goethe, *Egmont,* in *Gedenkausgabe der Werke, Briefe, und Gespräche: Die Weimaren Dramen*, ed. Ernst Beutler (Zurich: Artemis Verlag), vol. 6, 53–54.

12. We have translated one of the poems that bear witness to Goethe's lost love for Lilli: "On the Lake."

13. "Erlkönig," in *Gedichte*, 107–9.

14. Johann Wolfgang von Goethe, *Wilhelm Meisters Lehrjahre*, in *Gedenkausgabe der Werke, Briefe, und Gespräche*, ed. Ernst Beutler (Zurich: Artemis Verlag, 1949), 155.

15. "Warum gabst du uns die tiefen Blicke," in *Gedichte*, 229.

16. Boyle, 354.

17. "Fünfte Elegie," in *Gedichte*, 405–6.

18. See *Purkinje's Vision: The Dawning of Neuroscience* by Nicholas J. Wade and Josef Brožek in collaboration with Jiří Hoskovec, Lawrence Erlbaum Associates, Mahwah, New Jersey, 2001, 1–2 and *passim*.

19. John R. Williams, *The Life of Goethe: A Critical Biography* (Oxford: Wiley-Blackwell, 1998), 46.

Selected Poems

Note

The symbol ★ is used to indicate stanza breaks lost to pagination.

Epigraph for an Introduction to *The West-East Divan*

He who poetry would know
Into poem–land must go;
He who would the poets know
Into poet–land must go.

The Luck of Love

Drink, O youth, that daylong blessing
Of your loved one's eyes' possessing,
Nightly rocked by her sweet dream;
There's no lover had it better,
Yet your luck is ever greater
When she's far away, I deem.

Time and space, eternal forces,
Like the stars in secret courses,
Lull this blood with rockabye.
Passion will be daily slighter,
Yet my heart shall be the lighter,
And my luck will grow thereby.

Nowhere can I now forget her,
Yet in peace I eat without her
In a spirit light and free.
And a hidden coruscation
Turns my love to admiration,
Lust to sensitivity.

Not the lightest cloud, drawn higher
By the sun in warm desire,
Swims in such ethereal breath
As my heart in peace and pleasure.
Free of fear and envy's measure,
Now I love her beyond death.

1769–70

Dedication

to the recipient of a collection of early poems

So here they are! You have them now!—
These artless, toil-less songs somehow
Sprung from a brookside meadow.
With youth's sweet pain, in love, aflame,
I played the young man's ancient game,
And thus I sang its credo.

Sing, you who cannot help but sing
Upon a pretty day of spring;
And youth enlists their fable.
The poet squints, far off, for whom
Hygienic calm has pressed its thumb
Upon his parted eyeball.

Half cross-eyed and half wise, he peers—
Your bliss incites a few wet tears,
He wails in clause and meter.
He listens to his own good sense,
Supplying his best eloquence,
Knows the brief joys are sweeter.

You sigh, and sing, and melt, and kiss,
And shout with joy: the close abyss
Unknowingly disparage.
Escape the field, the sun, the rill,
Slink off, as if in winter's chill,
To seek the hearth of marriage.

*

You laugh at me and call me fool;
The fox who lost his tail would school
Us all to like curtailment.
But here the tale must surely fail:
This honest fox, snared by the tail,
Warns you from such beguilement.

1770

Maying

How nobly Nature
Shines upon me!
How the sun dazzles!
How laughs the lea!

Blossoms are bursting
From every bough,
A thousand voices
From each bush now,

And joy and pleasure
From every breast.
O Earth, O sunblaze!
O joy! O lust!

O love! O lovely!
So golden fair,
Like morning-nimbus
In mountain air.

How grand your blessings
On each fresh field—
In flower-vapor
The world revealed!

Girl, how I love you,
Just utterly!
How your eye flashes!
How you love me!

*

Just as the lark loves
Air and sweet cry,
And morning-blossoms
The scent of sky,

So I love you, love,
With blood's warm dart,
Who gives me youth
And joy and heart

For songs unwritten,
Dances to be.
Be always happy,
In love with me!

1771

Welcome and Farewell

My heart beat hard, I sprang to saddle!
The deed was done before the thought.
Night rocked the earth in its soft cradle,
And on the mountains hung the night;
The oak in foggy mantle towered
A giant in the dimming skies,
Where darkness from the bushes glowered
Out of a hundred deep black eyes.

The moon from a great cloud-hill looking
Gazed sadly through a fragrant haze,
The breezes beat their soft wings, plucking
With dreadful rufflings at my ears.
The night shaped forms of monstrous direness,
Yet fresh and joyous was my mood:
For in my veins was such a furnace,
And in my heart such fire and blood!

I saw you, and a gentle sweetness
Flowed from your glance into my soul;
My heart in you found such completeness,
And every breath made you its goal.
A rosy-tinted springtime weather
Played round your face's lovely curve,
And love for me—ye Gods!—whatever
I hoped for, I did not deserve!

But ah, the sun, already rising,
Tightened the farewell in my heart:

What joy was in your kiss, amazing!
What pain was in your eyes, what smart!
I left, you stood there earthward gazing,
Then stole a moist glance after me:
But to be loved, what joy past praising,
And—Gods!—to love, what ecstasy!

1771

Wild Rose

Once a boy a wild rose spied,
Rosebud in the heather;
Young and fresh as morningtide,
Ran to see, all eager-eyed,
Joyful, gazing thither.
Rosebud, rosebud, rosebud red,
Rosebud in the heather.

Then the boy said: I'll pick you,
Rosebud in the heather!
Rosebud answered: I'll prick you,
I'll not be forgot by you:
I'll not bear it either.
Rosebud, rosebud, rosebud red,
Rosebud in the heather.

And the rude lad plucked her then,
Rosebud from the heather;
Rosebud pricked him, but in vain
Was for her all grief and pain,
She must ache forever.
Rosebud, rosebud, rosebud red,
Rosebud in the heather.

1771

The New Amadis

When that I was but a boy,
Locked up on my own,
Many years I spent that way
Just as if alone
In my mother's womb.

You were then my waking dream,
Golden fantasy;
And the ardent hero I,
Just like Prince Pipí,
Errant, ventured by.

Crystal castles I had wrought,
And destroyed them too;
And into the dragon's gut
My bright spear I threw.
What a man I'd be!

Chivalrous I now set free
That fair fish-princess,
Who with *parfit courtoisie*
Led me to the *messe*
In my gallantry.

Bread of heaven was her kiss,
Glowing as the wine—
Ah, I almost died of this.
Mailed with sunblaze like a shrine,
Glorious was she.

Who has stolen her from me?
Did some magic band
Hold her back from liberty?
Where's her native land?
Where's the path? Tell me.

1771–74

Wanderer's Storm Song

Not rain, nor storm,
Can shake his heart
Whom you have not forsaken, Genius.
Against the hailstorm,
Against the cloud-wrack
He whom you have not deserted
Will be singing
Like the lark, Genius,
O you on high!

Whom you never leave, O Genius,
On fiery wings you will raise him up
Above the muddy path;
He will wander
Flower-footed
Over the ooze of Deucalion's inundation;
Python shall he destroy, light, great,
Pythian Apollo.

Whom you never leave, O Genius,
You will bear up with your fleecy wings
Where he sleeps upon the rock,
Cover him with guardian-pinions
In the midnight's darkest grove.

Whom you never leave, O Genius,
You in deepest snow will
Warmly swaddle;
To what's warm bow down the muses,
To what's warm bow down the graces.

★

Hover around me, Muses! Graces!
This is water, that is earth,
And, the son of water and the earth,
I am free to wander
As a god.

Pure you are, as the heart of water,
Pure as the earth's aeon-deep marrow;
You hover round me and I hover
Over earth, and over water,
As a god.

Does that little peasant,
Fiery, sunburned, ever retreat?
Turn back, though all he hopes in reward
Be but your gifts, good Father Bromius,
And a bright-glowing warm hearth-fire,
Brave in his return?
Should I, then, your companion,
One whom the Muses and the Graces
All await in expectation,
Whose life Muses and Graces
Glorified with wreaths of bliss,
Now turn back disheartened?

Father Bromius!
Genius you are too,
Genius of centuries;
That inner fire
Of Pindar;
To the world,
Phoebus Apollo.

Woe, woe! That inner glow,
Warmth of the soul,
Center it!
Glow, fire, back at
Phoebus Apollo;
Else cold be
His princely glance,
Gliding over you uncaring,
Struck with envy,
Lingers on the mighty cedar
Not delaying
In its greening.

Why does my song name you last?
You from whom it began,
You in whom it ends,
You from whom it wells out,
Jupiter Pluvius!
You, you, my song jets forth,
Jupiter Pluvius,
You from whose Castalian Spring
This tributary stream
Flows idly on
In mortal happiness;
You who hold and protect me,
Jupiter Pluvius!

Not by the elm tree
—Storm-breathing deity!—
Did you ever visit
Him who cradled in his arms

That pair of doves,
Wreathed with the amiable rose,
Playful, flower-rejoicing,
Anacreon.
Nor in the poplar grove
By the shores of Sybaris
On the tall mountainside
Upon whose brow shines the Sun,
Did you ever embrace
That bee-singing,
Honey-bubbling one
Who waves in greeting,
Theocritus.

When the chariots rattled,
Wheel to wheel, toward the finish line,
High flew the whipcrack
Of youth inflamed with victory;
The dust whirled
As down from the mountain
Whirl the hailstones of the storm;
Your soul burned, Pindar,
Always toward dangers
—Courage, Pindar—glowed,
Poor heart!
There on the hill,
Heavenly power!
But there's enough fire
—Yonder is my hut—
To trudge all the way there.

1772

Mahomet's Song

Look! The rock-brook,
Bright-delighting,
Like a star glints!
Over cloudmists
Genial spirits
Fed his boyhood
Through the cliff-walls in the thickets.

Fresh as youth,
From clouds he dances
Down onto his marble stonebed,
Shouts again to
Have his heaven.

Through the mountain highroads
Hunts he after piebald pebbles,
His precocious captain-stride
Wrenching all his brother-brooklets
Down along him.

Lower now grow in the vale
Flowers underneath his footsteps,
And the meadows
Live upon his breath.

Yet no shadow-valley holds him,
Not a flower
Clinging to his knees can keep him,

Flattering with love-eyes longing;
To the plains his course he urges,
Snake-meandered.

Streams will yield them
To him gladly; steps he now
Into flatlands silver-shining
And the flatlands shine with him,
And the rivers of the plainlands
And the runnels of the mountains
Shout with him and call out: Brother,
Brother, take your brothers with you,
All along to your old father,
To the great eternal sea,
Who with open arms embracing
Waits for us;
Ah, but still in vain they open
To receive the yearners for him;
For the barren wastes devour us,
Greedy sands, the sun above us,
Swallow up our blood,
Or a hill will
Hem us in to make a lake. Brother,
Lead the brothers from the flatlands,
Take the brothers from the mountains
With you to your father now!

Come, you all!—
And now he swells him
Grandly, a whole generation
Bears the Prince high up aloft.

And in rolling triumph riding
Gives he names to countries, cities
Spring up underneath his feet.

Irresistibly he rushes,
Leaves behind him flaming towers,
Fire-peaked marble mansions, shapings
Of his masterful abundance.

Atlas carries cedar-houses
On his giant shoulders, soughing
Waft above his lofty head
Sails in thousands to the heaven
Of his might and of his glory.

And so carries he his brothers,
Those his treasures, those his children,
To his waiting all-begetter,
Joy a whirlwind in his heart.

1772–73

Prometheus

Eclipse and cloud your heavens, Zeus,
With fogs and mists!
And practice, like a boy
Who lops the thistles,
Beheading oaks and mountain peaks!
Leave my Earth alone, though;
You must let stand
My little hut
That you did not build,
And my own hearth
For whose bright glow
You envy me.

I know nothing more wretched
Under the sun than you, you gods!
Miserably do you feed
With taxed burnt offerings
And whispered prayers
Your Majesties,
And would starve, were not
Children and beggars
Still such hopeful fools.

When I was a child
Knowing not out from in,
I turned my errant eye
Up to the sun as if there were
An ear to hear my lamentations,
A heart like mine
Swelling with pity for the overburdened.

Who helped me then
Against the Titans' arrogance?
And who delivered me from death,
From slavery?
Holy and glowing heart, did you not
Accomplish it yourself?
And glowed too, young and good,
Swindled, salvation-thankful to
The Sleeping One above?

I honor thee? What for?
Did ever yet you salve the pains
Of the afflicted?
Have you ever stilled the tears
Of those who are terrified?
Was I not forged into a man
By almighty Time
And by eternal Fate,
My masters, and yours too?

Was it your will,
Perhaps, that I should hate life,
Flee into deserts,
Because not all
My boy-mornings
Could ripen into flower-dreams?

Here sit I, fashion humans
After my own image,
A race that, like me,
Can suffer, can weep,

Can savor, can rejoice,
And will no more revere you
Than do I.

1773

Ganymede

Like a rosy dawn
You ring me with your glow,
O darling Spring!
With blisses thousandfold
You urge into my heart
The holy fervor
Of your eternal warmth,
O you unending beauty!

That I might embrace you
In these arms!

Ah, on your breast
I lie, I languish,
And your flowers, your meadows
Press in upon my heart.
You cool the burning
Thirst in my bosom,
Loveliest morning-wind!
And the nightingale still calls
To me, amorous, out of the misty vale!

I come, I come!
But where? Ah, where?

Up there! Upward, upward,
The clouds float up,
Bearing it up, the clouds,
Tending this yearning love.

To me, to me!
In your lap, O clouds,
Upward!
Embracing, embraced,
Upward to your bosom,
All-loving Father!

1774

The King in Thule

Unto the King in Thule,
Faithful beyond the grave,
His dying sweetheart truly
A golden goblet gave.

This cup, his greatest treasure,
At every feast he'd drain;
His tears, beyond all measure,
Flowed time and time again.

And when his last he's breathing,
He counts his cities up,
All worldly goods bequeathing,
But not the precious cup.

His knights all ranged around him,
He dines full solemnly,
In those high halls that crowned him,
His castle by the sea.

Old drinker in his palace,
He stood, drank life's last glow,
And threw the sacred chalice
Into the flood below.

He saw it fall, and drinking,
Founder into the main.
His eyes, too, now are sinking;
He never drank again.

1774

To Cousin Kronos, the Coachman

(in a post-chaise, Oct.10, 1774)

Crack on, coachman!
Whip up a rattling trot!
Downhill glides the road;
My skull swims, sick-dizzy
With your dilly-dallying
Quick, never mind the bumps—
Over sticks and stones
Trot on, trot on into Life!

Again, again,
The gasping plod
Up the irksome hill!
Up then, don't dawdle,
Hopefully, hard-striving, upward!

All around now opens
Life's grand panorama,
Mountain to mountain
Floats the eternal spirit,
Foretaste of life eternal.

Under the eaves
A shadow beckons,
Fresh glance of promise,
Girl on the threshold.
Go get yourself a drink!
A foamy one for me too, girl!
A fresh health to my friend!

Down then, downhill faster!
See where sinks the sun!
Quick, before it sinks, before
Gray-headedness grips me—
Fog-scent of the fens,
Toothless jaws achatter,
A dangle of clattering bones.

Drunk with the last day-ray,
Tear me away, fire-sea
In my flaming eye,
Blinded, dizzy, into
Hell's midnight gates.

Sound your horn, coachman,
Rattle the ringing trot,
Let Orcus hear it; we come, we come,
And there at the threshold
The host welcomes us in.

1774

On the Lake

And now I suck fresh life and blood
From this free world expressed;
How lovely Nature is, how good,
Holding me at her breast!
The deep wave rocks our rowboat's boards
In measure with the oars,
And mountains clouded heavenwards
Meet with us on our course.

Eyes, my eyes, why are you falling,
All your golden dreams recalling?
Hence, you dreams! For all your gold,
Love and life are here to hold.

On the wave there glimmer
Thousands of hovering stars,
And a blue-mist shimmer
Swallows the mountain-towers;
Winds of dawn are gliding
'Round the shadowy cove,
And in its mirror riding,
Fruit ripens in the grove.

1775

The Artist's Evening Song

Ah, may the making power ring
Within my mind's wide spaces,
And may a sap-filled growing spring
Forth from my fingers' traces!

I only stutter, only quake,
But cannot throw you over:
Nature, I've loved you for your sake,
Must cleave to you forever.

I think how many a long year
My mind's confines expanded,
How in that barren heath and drear
Joy's wellsprings made it splendid;

Nature, in mine I'd see your face,
Truth, love, your simple glories!
Your merry water-jets and sprays
A thousand capillaries.

And so may you on all my powers
Confer new elevation,
And stretch my narrow present hours
To endless aspiration.

1775

The Bliss of Grief

Dry them not, dry them not,
Tears of perpetual passion!
Ah! to the half-dry eye appears only
A world that is empty, desolate, dead!
Dry them not, dry them not,
Tears of unhappiest passion!

1775

Wanderer's Night Song (1)

You who are of heaven born
All man's griefs and torments stilling,
Him whom care has doubly worn
Doubly now with new life filling,
How I weary of life's labor!
Wherefore all this lust and smart?
Peace, sweet savior,
Come, ah come, into my heart!

1776

To Charlotte von Stein

Why did you grant us these premonitions,
Future visions we can never trust,
Blessings or—we cannot know—illusions:
Loves and joys of Earth's uncertain dust?
Fate, why did you give us these deep feelings,
That discern the other's secret heart,
In that wanton chaos, those revealings
Where our true bond takes its central part?

Ah, so many thousands know no better
Than to drift unpurposed to and fro
Numb to their own hearts, or, fleeing, scatter
Hopelessly in unprovided woe,
And rejoice when transient pleasure hovers
Dawning upon their unenlightenedness;
Only to this pair of wretched lovers
Is denied our mutual happiness:
The sweet dream of loving without knowing,
Seeing the other as she's never been,
Finding dream-joy always overflowing,
Whirled through perilous figments unforeseen.

Happy he whose dream is all his passion!—
Who believes his visions, though in vain!
If our glances, meetings, give permission,
Ah, the more our future-dreams ordain.
Say, what fate is even now preparing,
Say, how first it bound us, life to life?
In some former age that we were sharing,
You were my own sister, or my wife!

You discerned each fraction of my being,
Heard the music of its purest string,
Read me with your piercing art of seeing,
One for mortal eyes no easy thing;
In hot blood you trickled moderation,
Ruled the helter-skelter of the chase;
In the angel arms of consolation
Nursed the wounded breast that sought your grace;
You with weightless magic bonds restrained him,
Sometimes tricked him gently from his aim;
What delight can match those hours that chained him,
Prostrate at your feet, grateful and tame?
Now he feels his heart on yours is swelling,
As it once felt happy in your eyes;
All his senses light up with the feeling,
But his mad blood, calmed, forgets to rise.

Most of all a memory drifts stealing
Just around the strange uncertain heart;
Ancient truth eternally indwelling,
But renewed, is felt as grievous smart.
Half-ensouled we seem in our reflections,
Darkling seems the light of the daystar;
Happy, though, that fate with its afflictions
Will not make us other than we are.

1776

34

Restless Love

Through snow, through shower,
The wind's wild power,
Through steaming gorges'
Fog-scented surges,
Ever on, ever on!
Rest and peace are gone!

I'd rather suffer,
Struggle and battle,
Than for life's offer,
Happiness, settle.
All of those passions,
Heart-to-heart ferment—
How the self fashions,
Ah, its own torment.

Can I, poor creature,
Flee back to nature?
All is in vain!
You are the crown,
Joy without peace,
Love—never cease!

1776

Winter Journey in the Harz

As the falcon
Resting on the heavy dawn-cloud
With his downy pinions
Seeks his prey,
So my song should hover.

For a god has
Charted out already
For each his own way,
Where who is lucky
Hurries swiftly
To his joyous goal:
But he whose heart
Is shrunken with bad luck
Struggles in vain
Against the bonds
Of that brazen cord
That's only to be severed
By the bitter shears.

Into the rainswept thicket
The wild beasts plunge,
And with the sparrows
The rich too have sunk
Into the common mire.

Easy it is to follow the wain
Driven by Fortuna,
Like the comfortable crowd

On the road of preferment
Behind the Prince's progress.

But who's that over there?
His path is lost in the thorn-brakes,
Behind him the branches
Rebound together,
The grass stands up again,
The wasteland swallows him.

Ah, who shall heal his torment?
For whom his balm becomes poison,
Who has drunk the hatred of men
Out of the fullness of love?
First scorned, now scorning,
In secret he eats up
His own self-worth
In his insatiate self-quest.

If in your book of psalms,
Father of Love, there is one note
That his ears can hear,
Quench then his heart with it!
Open his cloudy sight
To the thousand springs
That are so close to the thirsty one
In the desert!

You who shape such joys
To each his overflowing portion,
Bless the brotherhood of the hunt
On the track of deadly game

With youthful exuberance,
With merry bloodlust,
Avengers, at last, of injuries
For years resisted in vain
By the staves of the countryfolk.

But hide that lonely one
In your cloud of gold!
Till the rose blooms once more,
Shelter with winter evergreens
The rain-soaked hair, O Beloved One,
Of your poet!

With a twilight torch
You light his way
Across the night ford,
Upon unfounded ways,
Across empty fields;
With the thousand-hued dawn
You are laughing into his heart;
With the bitter storm
You bear him into the heights;
Winter torrents plunge from the crags
In his psalms,
And the dreadful summit
Is for him the altar
Of loveliest thanksgiving,
Its crown hung with snow
And wreathed with strings of spirits
By a propitiating people.

Revealed you stand
With unfathomable heart

Mysterious over the marveling world
And gaze from your clouds
On their riches and glory
That from the veins of your brothers beside you
You water with your streams.

1777

To the Moon

Groves and vales you fill once more
With your soft mist-shine,
Loosing, as so long before,
All this soul of mine;

Over all my fields you send
Your assuaging glance,
Like the mild eye of a friend
On my life's forechance.

Every echo my heart feels
Wakes times ill and good;
I, between old woes and weals,
Roam in solitude.

Run, dear river, ever run!
Joy will never stay,
Jests and kisses, faith too, spun
Murmuring away.

Once I held what after all
Most is to be prized!
—Grief which, unforgettable,
Never is excised.

Rush, stream, down the vale along,
Without rest or ease;
Rushing, whisper to my song
Riven melodies,

When you in the winter night
Raging overflow,
Or around the young buds bright
Gush with springtime's glow.

Happy he who, grudgeless, best
Locks the world away,
Holds one dear friend to his breast,
With him to enjoy

What, to humankind unknown
Or not brought to light,
Through heart's labyrinth alone
Wanders in the night.

1777

All Things the Gods Bestow

All things the gods bestow, the unending ones,
To their darlings, all,
All joys, the unending ones,
All pains, the unending ones, all.

1777

Take This to Heart

Ah, what should be man's desiring?
Better still in peace remaining?
Hanging fast and not aspiring?
Better driving, striving, straining?
Should one build a cozy dwelling?
Be a tented nomad, drifting?
Trust a rock, to keep from falling?
Even steadfast rocks are shifting.

No command is sent to all:
Let each see what he is doing,
Choose his fastness still unmoving;
And who stands, stands lest he fall.

1777

The Fisherman

The water whispered, swelled, and flowed,
An angler sat embarked;
He gazed and gazed upon his rod,
And peace was in his heart:
But as he sits and listens there,
The rustling flow divides,
And from the river, wet and bare,
A woman upward glides.

She sang, she spoke: Why do you snare
With human tricks and lies
My finny brood into the glare
Of your hot deadly skies?
Ah, would you knew how fit a home
My fishes find their bed,
Then as you are, you'd yield and come
There, where you're healed and fed.

Do not our own dear moon and sun
Bathe themselves in the sea?
—And having breathed the waves, return
With doubled brilliancy?
Does not deep heaven lure you in,
That wet transcending blue—
Your own reflected face within
Its clear eternal dew?

The water whispered, swelled, and flowed,
Drenched his bare foot with bliss;

His heart yearned with its heavy load,
As with a lover's kiss.
She spoke, she sang, so cunningly,
It was the angler's bane:
Half-drawn by her, half-sinking, he
Was never seen again.

1778

Song of the Spirits upon the Waters

The soul of man
Is like the water:
From the sky it comes,
To the sky it goes
And down again
It must to the earth,
Changing ever.

In a limpid jet
It streams from the high
Steeps of the rockwall,
Sprays lovingly
In waves of cloud
Upon glossy stone;
And accepted lightly
Undulates in veils
Soft-murmuring
To the depths below.

Cliffs stand out
Against the crashing,
Foams it fiercely
Step by step
Down to the abyss.

In a level bed
It steals through the meadows
And in a glassy lake
All the constellations
Feast on their faces.

★

The wind to the wave
Is a sweet lover;
Wind stirs from the lakebed
Foaming surges.

Soul of mankind,
How like to the water!
Fate of mankind,
How like to the wind!

1779

Song of the Parcae

(from Goethe's play *Iphigenie auf Tauris*)

Well may the Divine Ones
Be feared by the race of man!
The gods hold dominion
In hands everlasting
And know how to use it
However they wish.

He doubly should fear them
Whom they have raised highest!
On cliffs and on cloud tops
Are chairs set out ready
Around golden tables.

Dissension arises;
The guests are ejected,
Are shamed and dishonored,
Cast down into nightfall,
Kept fruitlessly waiting
Enchained in darkness
For justice and judgment.

The gods, though, remain there,
Still endlessly feasting
At those golden tables.
They stride still from mountain
To mountain untroubled—
While from the abysses
Yet steams the gasped breathing

Of strangling Titans,
The waft of burnt offerings
In light floating clouds.

Those lords have averted
The eyes of their blessing
From their ancient kindred;
Refuse in the grandson
To see the once-cherished
Still-eloquent features
That sired the whole line.

And so sang the Parcae.
The exile, the old one,
In caverns of midnight,
Thinks, hearing their singing,
Of his child, of his child's children,
And then shakes his head.

1779

Wanderer's Night Song (2)

The high peaks everywhere
Are still;
Scarcely a breath of air
You feel
Up in the treetops there:
The birds have fallen silent too.
Wait for that peace, wait still:
It comes for you.

1780

Night Thoughts

O, you sad-souled stars, it's you I pity,
You so fair, shining majestically,
You the beacon to the hard-pressed sailor,
Unrewarded still by gods or mortals—
Why? Because you cannot love, nor know love.
Unrelentingly the hours eternal
Lead your ranks across the open heavens,
What a voyage have you since completed;
While within my lover's arms delaying,
You and midnight I have quite forgotten!

1781

Human Limitations

When the ancient
Holy father
With careless hand
From rolling clouds
Sows on the earth
His blessed lightnings,
I kiss the trailing
Hem of his dress,
A childish shudder
True in my breast.

For with gods
Never should man
Dare him to measure.
Should he heave himself up
And brush with his topknot
The stars of heaven,
His uncertain soles
Will find no purchase,
And clouds and winds
Will make him their plaything.

If he stands
With sturdy bones
On the founded
Enduring ground,
He'll never aspire
To liken himself
To anything higher
Than oak or vine.

What distinguishes
Gods from humans?
The waves that spread
From gods sweep outward
Ever-surging;
Those waves can lift us,
Tangle, whelm us,
And so we drown!

A little ring
Limits our life;
Many generations
Link up forever
In their being's
Eternal chain.

1781

My Goddess

To which of the deathless
Should the prize be given?
I quarrel with none,
But I bestow it
On that ever-moving,
Ceaselessly fresh,
Strangest daughter of Jove,
His lap-child,
Fantasy.

For unto her
He has granted
All changes of mood
That otherwise he reserves
To himself alone,
And his pleasure is
In the mad one.

Oft she steps
Garlanded with roses
And the tall-stemmed lily
Into the flower vales,
And tells the summer birds
To suck with their bee lips
The nourishing dew
From the blossoms;

Oft does she
With flying hair

And darkling looks
Rush with the wind
About the crags
And thousand-tinted
As dawn and eve,
Changing eternally,
As seems the moon,
Reveal herself to mortals.

    May all of us
Praise the Father,
The old one on high,
Who a wife so lovely
And so unfading
Has joined to our
Mortal humanity!

    For to us alone
Has he bound her
With the bonds of heaven,
And bade her
Whether in joy or grief
As a true wife
Never to waver.

All the other
Unluckier breeds
Of the living Earth
So rich in progeny
Wander and graze
In the dim pleasure
And somber pain

Of a brief, blinkered,
And shrunken existence
Bent under the yoke
Of harsh necessity.

But he has granted us
That we might meet—Rejoice!—
The ablest and most cherished
Of all his daughters,
In close embrace
As we meet the beloved!
Allow her the dignity
Of a wife in her own house!

And that the old
Mother, Wisdom,
Offer no insult
To her delicate soul!

Yet I know her sister too,
The elder, the less unruly one,
My quiet friend:
O that only
With the light of life itself
Should she turn away from me:
The noble inspirer,
Comforter, Hope!

1781

The Elf-King

Who rides so late through wind and night?
A father with his child so white.
He holds the boy within his arm,
Hugging him fast to keep him warm.

"My son, why hide your face in fear?"
"D'you see the Elf-King, Father dear,
The Elven-King with cape and crown?"
"My son, 'tis fog upon the down."

"Sweet child, come with me now away;
Such lovely games we two will play,
Such lovely flowers upon the strand,
And golden robes from my mother's hand."

"Father, Father, don't you hear
What the Elf-King whispers in my ear?"—
"Be still, my child, and pay no mind:
'Tis dry leaves rustling in the wind."

"My fine lad, won't you come with me?
My daughters will serve you charmingly;
My daughters will dance our nightly rings
And lullaby your slumberings."

"Father, Father, can't you see
The Elf-King's daughters on the dark lea?"
"My son, my son, I see it clear:
'Tis but old willows hoar and drear."

"My boy, I love your form so well,
That if you come not, I can compel!"
"Father, Father, he has me fast!
The Elf-King scathes me with his blast!"—

The father in horror rides like the gale,
In his arms the moaning child so pale,
He comes to the house in toil and dread:
But in his arms the child is dead.

1782

Divinity

Be noble, humankind,
Merciful and good!
For that alone
Marks him off
From all beings
That we know.

Hail to those unknown
Higher beings
We can only guess!
In man's image and likeness,
By their example
We are taught to believe.

Because Nature
Is all-unfeeling;
The sun gives light
To the good and the wicked,
And on the best man
So on the felon
Shine the moon and the stars.

Winds and storms,
Thunder and hail
Rumble on their way
And careless in their haste
They catch in their grip
One man with another.

*

Just so fortune
Gropes among the crowd,
Seizes now the boy's
Curled innocence,
Now the bald pate
Of the guilty man.

By great eternal
Immutable laws
Must we fulfill
The natural cycles
Of our being.

But man alone
May do the impossible:
He makes distinctions,
Chooses, judges;
He can to the moment
Grant permanence.

He alone may
Reward the good,
Punish the evil,
Heal and save
All that's in error,
Use and connect.

And so we honor
Those the undying ones
As if they were human
Acting in great things
As the best man in small things
Does, or desires to do.

Noble humanity
Be good and merciful!
Create untiringly
The useful, the righteous,
Be for us an image
Of those guessed beings!

Early 1780s

"Joyful and Woeful . . ."
from *Egmont*

Joyful
And woeful
And brooding in vain;
Longing
And fearing,
Suspended in pain;
Sky-high elated
And dying with rue,
Happy alone
Is the soul that loves true.

1788

Morning Complaints

O you wicked careless heartless darling,
Tell me wherein I've been found out guilty,
That upon the rack you thus should stretch me,
That your given word you should have broken?

And you pressed my hand last night, so friendly,
Lisped to me your promise O so sweetly,
"Yes, I'll come to you, depend upon it,
Dearest friend, I'll meet you in your chamber."

So I left my double doors unfastened,
Having checked the hinges' operations,
Pleased they had no creak that could betray us.

What a night of waiting then has followed!
I kept stirring, tried to count the quarters;
Even if I slept a few brief minutes,
My poor heart was constantly awakened,
Roused me always from my gentle slumbers.

Yes, I blessed the secret gift of darkness,
Which discreetly covered all in quiet,
Happy in that universal silence,
Listening intently to the stillness,
If the slightest sound might now be stirring.

"Had she had such thoughts as I imagine,
Had she felt the feelings that possessed me,
She would not have waited for the morning:
By this hour she would have come already."

Now a kitten pounces in the attic,
And a quick mouse skitters in the corner,
Something rustles somewhere in the building.
Always I had hope to hear your footstep,
Always I believed I'd hear your footstep.

So I lay in long and ever longer,
And the day already started graying,
Here there was a rustle, there a rustle.

"Can that be her door? Would it were *my* door."
In my bed I sat up quick, bolt upright,
And was peering at the half-lit doorway,
Whether she was moving there behind it.
But both door-wings only stayed half-open,
Hanging silently upon their hinges.

And the day got light and ever lighter,
I'd already heard my neighbor's door latch,
In his hurry to get off to business.
Soon I heard the rattle of the hackney,
So the city gates must have been opened,
And the whole pantechnicon got going,
All the marketplace's toing, froing.

In the house too, people coming, going,
Up and down the stairs, backward and forward,
Doors were squeaking, footfalls ran a-patter;
Still I would not from my hopes divorce me
Than from all the beauty of existence.

When at last the sun, hated by lovers,
Met my windows and my walls together,
I jumped up and hurried to the garden,
Mingling my hot breath of pent-up yearning
With the airy coolness of the morning,
Maybe then to meet you in the garden:
But you're neither in the hidden arbor
Nor in the high avenues of lindens.

1788

Five Roman Elegies

I

Speak, O stones of Rome! Whisper to me, you high palaces;
Streets, breathe me a word! City-soul, do you not stir?
Yes, within your holy ramparts all is enspirited,
Roma aeterna, all that's around me has hushed till it's still.
Ah, who whispers to me?—in which window will first I
    encounter
That glance, that exquisite form that will quicken and burn?
Little do I suspect the ways by which ever, and ever
I'm drawn to and from her, sacrifice all the delights of my time.
Yet do I contemplate palace and temple, ruin and column
Quite as a wiser, more circumspect traveler might on his tour.
Soon, though, it will be over, then will one single temple,
Amor's temple, receive its initiate, be his alone.
Though you are indeed the world, O Rome, yet if love were
    lacking,
This world would not be this world, neither would Rome be
    Rome.

1788–90

III

Do not regret, beloved, how swift you believe your surrender;
Know that with you no impertinent baseness colors my thoughts.
Many the ways of the arrows of Amor; one merely scratches,
And its poison, secretly creeping, sickens the heart through the
    years.
But mightily fletched, with keen and freshly honed edges
The others strive to the core and set us at once aflame.
When gods and goddesses loved, in the ancient time of the
    heroes,
Lust would follow the glance, and pleasure followed desire:
Do you think that the goddess of Love would ever think twice
    for a moment
When in the forests of Ida Anchises attracted her eye?
Had Luna that night hesitated to kiss the beautiful sleeper
O, how swiftly would he have been woken by envious Aurora!
Hero espied Leander in the midst of the raucous festival
And nimbly the feverish lover plunged in the midnight flood.
Rhea Sylvia wanders, the princely virgin, down to the Tiber
Its water to draw in her ewer, but instead a god scoops her up.
So by Mars two sons are begotten!—the twins are suckled
At she-wolf's teats; and Rome names herself princess of the
    world.

1788–90

67

V

Happy I find myself now on the soil of the classical landscape;
Times past and present speak out more boldly and sweetly to
　me.
Here I take as my guide the pages once penned by the
　ancients,
Leafing with busy hand through their works with a daily
　delight.
Yet in the night Amor is keeping me busy quite otherwise;
Though it's but half my tuition, my joy is multiplied twice.
Do I learn nothing then when I study the lovely ensculpting
Rounding that bosom, the curve of my hand as it traces her
　hips?
Then do I rightly conceive of the marble; contemplate,
　measure,
See with the eyes of touch, and feel with such seeing hands.
Thus if my darling robs from me certain hours of daylight,
Hours of night she gives me to pay for the cost of the theft.
No, it's not kissing alone that goes on—there is rational
　discourse;
She being conquered by sleep, I lie there envolumed with
　thoughts;
Often within her arms I've written the poem already,
Counted with fingering hand along the line of her spine
Softly the measured hexameter. She breathes in lovely slumber,

Breath that glowingly penetrates into the depth of my breast.
Amor trims the lamp and thinks of the many ages,
Musing upon the triumvirs, they whose will he once served.

1788–90

VII

How merry I am in Rome! I remember the mood of the days
When a miserable grayness immured me at home in the North,
Dreary the overcast sky weighed down on my skull forever,
Round one's exhausted being a formless and colorless world.
Over the I, my I, immersed in deepening gloominess,
Brooded and peered, down the dark paths of the soul.
Now, though, my brow is lit by a glittering halo of ether,
Phoebus has come, invoking the glory of color and form.
Starlight englitters the night, it echoes with music and singing,
And to me here the moon shines brighter than once did the
    light of the day.
What bliss was mortal being? Am I dreaming? Father Jupiter,
How can it be that your perfumy mansion receives this guest?
Ah, my lord, here I lie and stretch out in humble entreaty
My hands for your knees—O Jupiter Xenius, ask what you
    will!
How it was that I entered here I cannot say; Hebe
Gripped this wanderer, drew him into the innermost shrine.
Did you command her to fetch a hero in triumph?
Was the lovely one wrong? Forgive her! Allow me error's
    reward!
Your daughter, Fortuna, forgive her too! In girlish ardor
She gives out those glorious gifts as the thoughtless mood
    dictates.
Are you the god of hosts? O banish not then this affable
Guest and hurl him down from Olympus again to the earth.

"Poet, where did you lose your way on the climb?" Forgive me,
To you the Capitoline Hill a second Olympus must be.
Suffer my presence, Jupiter; at length let Hermes lead me
Lightly, by Cestius' pyramid, down to the vale of Orcus.

1788–90

X

Flames, autumnal, glow on the rustic sociable hearthstone,
Flaring so swiftly up from the kindling they crackle and blaze.
And what makes me happier still, before the twigs in their
    bundle
Burn down to embers and twistingly poke themselves into the
    ash,
Enters my lovely girl. Now kindling and logs blaze up freely,
And the warmed night becomes for us a glittering feast.
Busily then next morning she'll leave the camp of lovemaking
And, nimble, rouse from the ashes the freshly rekindled flame.
For above all other gifts does Amor grant us this flattery:
To arouse the spirit of joy that had almost sunk into cinders.

1788–90

The Nearness of the Beloved

I think of you, feeling the sun's bright shimmer
From the sea's blue;
When the moon's painted in the wellspring's glimmer
I think of you.

I see you when above the distant highway
The dust awakes;
When on the footbridge of the midnight byway
The traveler quakes.

I hear you when with sullen roaring violence
The wave-crest breaks;
In the still grove I listen for the silence
Your absence makes.

I am with you; however far you wander,
Still you are near.
The sun is setting, stars blaze out up yonder:
Would you were here!

1795

The Silent Sea

Deepest stillness rules the ocean,
Flat calm has subdued its face;
And the vast suspense of motion
Makes the sailor rue the place.
Not a breath from any quarter!
Deathly silence everywhere!
On the frightful endless water
Not a ripple stirs the air.

1796

Three Poems from *Wilhelm Meisters Lehrjahre*

"D'you know that land where lemon blossoms blow . . ."

This fairytale, how strange to you!—
But poetry can make it true.

"D'you you that land where lemon blossoms blow,
Where in dark leaves the orange gold-fruit glow,
Where the mild wind wafts from the azure sky,
The myrtle's still, the bayleaf shines on high—
Know you that land?"
                              "Ah there, ah there,
I yearn to go with you, my heart's desire."

"Know you the house?—its pillared portico,
Its glittering halls, its shining studio
Where marble forms stand up and meet your gaze?
Poor child, what trouble has beset your days?
Know it at all?"
                              "Ah there, ah there,
I yearn to go, under your loving care!"

"Know you that mountain with its cloud-choked ways
The mule seeks through the fog as in a maze,
Where the caves house the ancient dragon-brood
And the high cliffs thunder with the falling flood?
Know you that place?"
                              "Away, away!
O Father, take me, take me all the way!"

1795–96

"Ah, none but those who yearn . . ."

Ah, none but those who yearn
My pain can measure,
Unfriended and alone,
Reft of all pleasure,
Beneath the Milky Way
I strain to see him—
My love is far away;
I, left behind him.
I swoon, my innards burn,
I've lost my treasure;
Ah, none but those who yearn
My pain can measure!

1795–96

"Who never ate his bread with tears . . ."

Who never ate his bread with tears,
In nights unsleeping, unforgiven,
Weeping with grief and racked with fears,
Has never known you, powers of Heaven!

You lead us into life's domain,
You let the wretch transgress and injure;
And then you give him up to pain,
For all guilt is its own avenger.

1795–96

The Sorcerer's Apprentice

So the sly old necromancer
Toddles off and leaves me standing,
And his spirits all must answer
At my will and my commanding.
I have marked his actions,
Studied every spell,
And his strong projections
I can work as well.

Hubble-bubble
To each quarter
Let the water
Rush and flow;
And its surging flood redouble,
Rich and gushing high and low.

So, old broomstick, monkey-punky,
Clothe yourself with scarecrow tatters.
All these years you've been a flunky,
Now it's me in charge of matters.
Make two legs to scurry,
Now a head you've got.
Get a move on! Hurry!
Fetch the waterpot!

Hubble-bubble
To each quarter
Let the water
Rush and flow;

And its surging flood redouble,
Rich and gushing high and low.

See, he's running to the river,
There already! What a fellow!
And like lightning, quick as ever,
He is back with gush and billow.
Now the basin's brimming;
Off again he goes!
Pots and pans are swimming,
Bathtub overflows!

Stop it, stop it!
Yes, you're tough!
Drop it, drop it,
That's enough!
Oh, I knew it! Bloody hell!
I have just forgot the spell!

Yes, the spell!—that unbewitches
Any magical disaster!
Still he dashes and he fetches!
Please, be just the same old duster!
Now the flood is brimming
All around the walls,
Oooh, I'm almost swimming
In these waterfalls!

I must grab him,
No more waiting,
So I'll nab him—
Ouch! That's cheating!

Now I'm frightened! Miserere!
Oh, that look he gave was scary!

Spawn of Hell, you water-devil,
Would you let the whole house drown?
Every sill and every level
Pours with water streaming down.
What a wicked doom-stick,
That will not obey!
You were once a broomstick—
Wish you'd stayed that way!

Misbegot,
Now you'll catch it!
You'll be caught,
I've a hatchet:
If you're never going to stop,
Your old wood is for the chop.

Here he comes, still at his schlepping.
Hah, I'll knock you on your back!
Goblin, then you'll stop your hopping—
Meet this keen blade with a crack!
Nice hit! It's a double!
See, he's cut in two!
There'll be no more trouble,
I can breathe now. Phew!

No, oh no!
Both halves rise!
Oh, they grow
Their former size,

Ready to serve up more showers!
Help, oh help, you higher powers!

Off they scamper! Rushing, splashing,
Wetness pours down hall and stairs,
Dreadful floods of water crashing!
Lord and master! Hear my prayers!
Blessings! Here's the Master
I called the spirits' aid,
They caused this disaster—
Help! They won't be laid!

"To the corner,
Broom, and broom!
Take your former
Shape and room.
Only the old master may
Call you—and only to his way."

1797

The God and the Dancer

Hindu Legend

Mahadur, lord of creation,
That he might become as we,
Enters his sixth incarnation,
Feels our joy and agony.
Making this his humble dwelling,
All that comes to him, he bears;
Deems with human sight and feeling,
Whether he condemns or spares.

As a wayfarer, then, he has looked at the city,
Inspected the great and considered the petty,
And he leaves in the evening, and onward he fares.

On the outskirts of the city,
On his way into the wild,
He has seen a girl, a pretty
Cheek-bepainted lost slave-child.
"Greetings, maiden!" And her answer:
"I am honored. Wait for me."
"Who are you?" "I am a dancer
For this house of love you see."

She steps from the threshold, her cymbals are dinning,
Her body a bending slow circle she's spinning,
And gives him a garland—so graceful is she!

Softly flattering and praising,
She has coaxed him through the door;

"Now our home lamps will be blazing,
Handsome stranger, all the more.
Are you weary? Let me ease you,
Give your sore feet's care to me;
Have whatever that may please you,
Pleasure, peace, or gaiety."

She comforts his pains, though they are but a fiction,
The god smiles with pleasure; through deepest corruption
The truth of the human heart he can still see.

He demands her slave-subjection;
She takes on a brighter glow;
Her precocious arts, by action,
Soon become her nature now.
So emerges from the flower
By and by the dulcet fruit;
With obedience's power,
Love oft follows in pursuit.

To test more severely the one he's selected,
The knower of heights and of depths has elected
Sweet pleasure, and horror, and pain absolute.

And her rouged cheeks now he kisses,
And she's caught in love's birdlime,
And she feels those anguished blisses
And she cries for the first time;
To his feet she sinks, not seeking
Means of lust nor hopes of gain;
Ah! Her slackened limbs are aching,
Will's commands are all in vain.

And over the bed's oh-so-sweet celebration
The dark hours of night cast their veil of discretion,
So beautifully woven, so homely and plain.

Late it is before she slumbers,
Early wakens from her rest.
Something cold her heart encumbers:
Dead, the well-beloved guest!
Screaming she his corpse embraces,
Nothing can his life reclaim:
His stiff limbs, with solemn paces
Priests bear to a grave of flame.

She hears the priests' prayers, the funeral dirges,
In madness she runs through the crowd as it surges:
"Why haste to the pyre, love? And what is your name?"

At the bier she now falls, shrieking:
"Give me back my husband dear!—
Even if I must be seeking
In the deepest pit of fear.
Shall those limbs, all grace and splendor,
Fall to ashes, though divine?
But one night of sweet surrender
He was mine, and only mine!"

The priests go on chanting: "We carry the old ones
Who long have been wearying, late become cold ones,
But the young ones we carry gave never a sign.

"Listen to your priests' instruction:
This is not your husband's bier.

Dancing is your life's direction:
No wife-duty claims you here.
Body follows shade, in suttee,
To death's silent realms that wait;
It's the wife's own prize and duty
So to seek her husband's fate.

"Then echo, you horns, the devout lamentation,
And take now, you gods, day's own pearl of creation,
And welcome this youth to the flames consecrate."

Thus the choir has mercilessly
Multiplied her heart's desire:
She with arms wide, effortlessly
Leaps into the grave of fire.
But the heavenly youth upsoaring
Lifts himself above the pyre,
In his arms her life restoring,
Wafts his darling higher and higher.

Now glad is the god for the sinner's contrition;
Immortals will lift a lost child from perdition
And bear her to heaven in arms of pure fire.

1797

The Bride of Corinth

Out of Athens came a youthful rover
Into Corinth, where he was unknown:
Hoping, for an ally, to win over
One of two fathers, friends, and one his own:
They had pledged to join
Daughter to the son
To be bride and bridegroom when they'd grown.

Will he, though, be welcomed in this bargain?
Can he buy the father's favor dear?
After all, his kin and he are pagan:
These are baptized Christians most sincere.
Where a new creed grows,
Often loves and vows
Like a noxious weed are torn out here.

But already the whole house is sleeping;
Only mother's up, and with a light
Entertains the guest with warm housekeeping,
Leads him to the room most grand and right.
Plied with food and wine,
He is called to dine;
Graciously she wishes him goodnight.

But before the meal so well assembled,
He is too tired for an appetite;
Into bed, full-clothed, he soon has tumbled,
Food and drink he cannot but forget;
Almost deep in rest,

When an unknown guest
Enters through a door left open yet.

For he sees, by his lamp's gentle glimmer,
Shyly step a maiden veiled and gowned
All in white, into the silent chamber,
Round her head, a black and golden band.
Him she now espies,
Frightened with surprise,
And she raises up a quick white hand.

"Am I in this house so much a stranger,
Not to be alerted to this guest?
Kept here in a cell as if a danger—
Ah, I am with shame quite overpressed!
Rest here, if you please,
On your couch at ease;
I shall leave now quickly, as is best."

"Lovely maiden, stay!" the boy beseeches,
Springs up swiftly from his place of rest:
"Ceres, see, and Bacchus give these riches:
You, dear girl, bring Amor to the feast!
You are pale with fear!
Dear one, let us here
See how glad the gods are at our tryst!"

"Keep away, young man, you are mistaken:
Pleasures have no property in me."
But the last step has, alas, been taken.
In the mother's sick delusion she,
Convalescent, swore

Youth and Nature were
Subject since to Heaven's sole decree.

And the old gods' gaily colored rabble
Void that house, left silent by the loss:
Heaven holds but One, invisible,
And a savior, worshipped on the cross;
Prey is slaughtered here,
Neither lamb nor steer,
But a ghastly human sacrifice.

And he asks, and weighs well each word of it,
So that not one fails to speak his soul:
"Can it be?—my bride, my one beloved,
Stands before me in this silent hall?
Mine may she be now!
For our fathers' vow
Begged a heavenly blessing on us all!"

"You, good soul, can never now possess me,
They for you my sister do decree;
While in that still cell my griefs oppress me,
In her arms, oh pray you, think of me,
Who thinks but of you,
Lovesick for you, who
In the earth full soon will buried be."

"No! In this flame let the pledge be given,
Hymen blazes here, shows us the way:
You'll lose neither joy nor me, by heaven,
Come, love, to my father's house away.
Darling, do not flee,

Celebrate with me
This unlooked-for feast and wedding day!"

Now they change love-tokens with each other,
Golden is the chain she gives him there,
And a silver chalice he will offer,
Peerless in its artistry, and fair.
"That is not for me,
But I make a plea
That you grant me one lock of your hair."

Dull the witching hour's reverberated,
And it seems that she is well and fine,
See, she gulps with pale lips and unsated,
One great draught of dark and blood-red wine:
But of wheaten bread,
Friendly offerèd,
She took not the smallest speck or sign.

To the youth she hands the cup of wine;
Quick, like her, he drinks it lustily,
Urging her love while quietly they dine;
Ah, how lovesick that poor heart must be!
But she still resists,
Pleading, he insists,
Till, in tears, upon the bed falls he.

Casts herself beside him now, that lady,
"Ah, I hate to see you tortured so!
But, alas, you'd quake to touch my body,
Feeling what I hid, nor let you know.
For your love of choice

Is as cold as ice,
Though as white and lovely as the snow."

With strong arms he seizes her in passion,
Lovers' youthful strength has him full-manned.
"I would warm you, as my dearest mission,
Were you from the grave, from the cold ground!"
Breath and kiss, and so,
Loving overflow!
"Do you burn now, do you feel me burned?"

Love now faster locks them both together,
Tears are mixed with lust in their wild quest;
Each is conscious only in the other,
Greedy she sucks the flame-breath from his breast.
Love, in him run mad,
Warms her gelid blood,
But no heart is beating in her chest!

Meanwhile in the passage slinks the mother,
Busy late with domesticity;
Listens through the door where they're together,
Listens long, for what can these sounds be?
Plaint, delirium,
Bride and her bridegroom,
And the stammer of love's ecstasy.

At the door she stays awhile, unmoving,
For she would convince herself of this;
And she hears the high vows, fierce and loving,
Words of passion and dear emphasis.
"Hush! The rooster's crow!

It is time to go:
Will you come tomorrow?"—kiss on kiss.

Now the mother's wrath no more can suffer,
She unlatches the familiar door:
"Is this house a place for whores who offer
Flesh to sate a stranger's hot desire?"
In that moment she
Can by lamplight see—
God!—it's her own child she glimpses there.

And the young man in a shocked reaction,
With the girl's own veil, with tapestry,
Seeks to shroud his sweetheart from detection,
But she twists away and struggles free;
As with spirit-might
Rises slow and white
Her long form from veil and drapery.

"Mother! Mother!"—empty words, mere traces;
"You'd begrudge me but one night so fair!
You drove me away from all warm places,
Have I only woken to despair?
Were you not content
That I, shrouded, went
To an early grave at your desire?

"But from that piled burden of confinement
My own right now drives me to be free.
Neither may your chanting priests' atonement
Nor can your blessing have weight with me;
Salt and water may

Not youth's fire allay;
Nor the cold earth quench love's victory.

"This young man to me was dedicated
When yet Venus' joyous temple stood.
But you, Mother, broke the word you plighted,
For a false, an alien vow of good!
But no god will hear
If a mother swear
To deny her daughter's hand and blood.

"From the grave I will be exiled ever,
Seeking out the good that should be mine,
Still to love the man now lost forever,
And to suck his hot heart's bloody wine.
He has had his turn,
Others now I'll burn,
And the young folk to this rage consign.

"Lovely youth! Your life is over, broken;
Now you'll perish from this world of air;
Keep the chain, my gift and my love-token,
But—I take that brown lock of your hair.
Look well, what I say:
Next dawn be it gray,
Only brown in that far place we'll share.

"Listen, Mother, to my last petition:
Build for me a fitting funeral pyre;
Open up that abject hut, my prison,
Lay to rest the lovers in the fire;

When the flame has spread,
Ashes glowing red,
Where the old gods are, we'll hasten there."

1797

The Metamorphosis of the Plants

You are perplexed, my love, by this thousandfold mixed profusion,
    Flowering tumultuous everywhere over the garden grounds;
So many names you are hearing, but one suppresses another,
    Echoing barbarously the sound it makes in the ear.
Each of their shapes is alike, yet none resembles the other,
    Thus the whole of the choir points to a secret law,
Points to a holy puzzle. I wish, lovely friend, I were able to
    Happily hand you at once the disentangling word!—
Watch now and be transformed, how bit by bit the plant-form,
    Guided stepwise, builds to emerge in blossom and fruit!
Out of the germ it unfolds, the moment the still and fertile
    Lap of the earth has lovingly let it go out into life,
There where the charm of light, the holy eternal mover
    Now ushers in the most delicate structures of burgeoning
        leaves.
This was a power that simply slept in the seed; a prototype
    Lay there closed and curled up in itself inside the husk,
Leaf and taproot and seed, as yet half-formed and colorless;
    Thus the dry kernel holds and protects the dormant life,
Then it gushes, heaving up, trusting to milder moistures,
    Lifts itself all at once out of the enveloping night.
Still, though, it simply retains the form of its first appearance,
    Thus the infant reveals and betrays itself under the plant.
Soon after that, a following impulse, renewing, throws upward
    Knot upon towering knot, in still the original shape.
Never the same, though; for always its self-generation is manifold,
    Always the following leaf, you see there, is fully informed:
Notched, expanded, and split into apex and branched divisions,
    That which in embryo rested curled up in the organ below.
Now it achieves for the first time its highly determined completion,

Which in some species can leave you astonished and awed.
Fretted and torn all over its mastlike and bristling surface,
     Now in full force appears the drive to be endlessly free.
Here, though, Nature with mighty hand halts the upbuilding,
     Leading it gently on until its full form is complete.
So with more measure it guides the sap and tightens the vessels,
     Suddenly blazoning out the pattern's more dainty effects.
Silently now the drive ebbs from the leading edges,
     Letting the vein of the stem build itself fully out.
Leafless and swiftly, though, rises the stalk in its greater elegance,
     Where the observer is drawn to a yet more miraculous form:
Ringed in a circle, each petal, in number defined or left open,
     Sets itself, smaller at first, by its twin that emerged before.
Crowding around the axle, the mounting cup comes to decision,
     Which, in its highest form, releases its color-bright crown.
Nature thus boasts now a nobler and fuller manifestation,
     Stepwise arraying organ on organ in ordered display.
Always you're freshly amazed when the flower on its stem, now open,
     Sways there above the slender scaffold of altering leaves.
Now, though, this splendor becomes a new shaping's annunciation,
     Yes, the bright-tinted petal feels the hand of God;
Swiftly it draws itself in, and then the tenderest structures
     Bifold strive to emerge, determined to make themselves one.
Intimate now they stand, the lovely couples together,
     Round the sacred altar in order arranging themselves.
Hymen floats nearby, and heavenly fragrances violently
     Pour their sweet and quickening odors all through the air.
Germ cells at once swell up now, each an individual,
     Lovingly wrapped in the waxing fruits of the mothering
        womb.
Here, then, Nature closes the ring of eternal forces;
     Still, a new one promptly fastens itself to the old,

So that the chain might extend itself onward all through the ages,
  And that the whole be revitalized, as is the single one.
Turn now, beloved, your eyes to these blooming and colorful
  multitudes,
   See how, perplexing no longer, they stir there in view of your
    soul!
Every plant announces, to you now, the laws eternal
  Every flower louder and louder is speaking with you.
You but decipher here the holy glyphs of the Goddess,
  Everywhere, though, you see her—in even their changing itself.
Slow crawls the caterpillar, in haste the butterfly flutters,
  Man the adaptable changes himself the foreordained form.
Think then also, my love, how from the germ of acquaintance
  Little by little in us a familiar dearness springs up,
Friendship unveils itself in power from our inner concealment,
  Till like Eros at last it procreates flower and fruit!
Think how soon these forms and those, in their manifold course
  of emerging,
   Gently have lent to our feelings the presence of Nature herself!
So then, rejoice—and rejoice for today! Love in its holiness
  Strives to the highest fruit of the same movement of thought,
Same outlook on things, in harmonic contemplation,
  Thus the pair make their bond, and find out a loftier world.

1799

World Soul

Share yourself out into all times and places
In this most holy feast!
Tear yourself through the intervening spaces,
Fill up the All, released!

You glide now in unmeasurable distance,
In the gods' blessed dream,
And shine anew in joyful coexistence
With that star-spangled stream.

Drive yourself then, like unresisted comets,
Away and yet away,
As through the labyrinth of suns and planets
You cut your headlong way.

You swiftly grasp for unformed earths to fashion,
And shape them, fresh and deep,
To fill them fecundly with life and passion,
In one great measured sweep.

Circling you trace out Time's arcane florescence
Within the ether's drift,
Prescribe to stone the splits that are its essence,
The strict forms of each rift.

Now all things with a heavenly volition
To find perfection strive:
The parched green seeks the water of fruition,
Each dust mote is alive.

Constrained within the loving paradoxes
Of night's moist dews and steams,
Now Paradise, with tinted pomps and fluxes
Outstretched before you, gleams.

See how a host of opulent forms now rises
To find that light so fair,
And in the happy woods your eye surprises
The first love-smitten Pair.

And soon wild striving's quenched in something holy,
Sweet glances mutual;
And life, most fair, with thanks receives most fully
The All back from the All.

1801

Nature and Art

Nature and art, that seemed to flee each other,
Now find each other, ere I'd scanned the matter;
And the antipathy has vanished altogether,
And drawn to both at once, I love both better.

And after all, there's but one true endeavor!
Only when first we bind ourselves, in hours
Of toil and soul to art, may nature ever
Kindle our heart with all its freeing powers.

Thus has all growth and learning its creation;
No spirit that's unbound may venture ever
Upon the purest, highest consummation.

Who seeks the great must gird himself together,
Showing his mastery in limitation,
And only law can set us free forever.

1802

Permanence in Change

Would I might those early blessings,
Ah, for but one hour hold fast!
But the west wind shakes the blossoms
Raining down in its warm blast.
Should I thank the leaves that follow
For their green shade's welcome pall?
Soon enough, now fallow-yellow,
Storms will ravage them in Fall.

Fruit is grasped before it's gotten:
Quickly haste to take your share!
Now it's ripe, and now it's rotten,
Others germinate right there;
Your sweet valley's changed forever
Every time it showers with rain;
And in the river, never never
Can you ever swim again.

As for you!—that rock-bound fastness
Seems now to materialize—
Rampart, palace, see its vastness
Evermore with changing eyes.
Vanished are the lips of sweetness
That once pleasured in a kiss,
Daring feet that tried their featness
Goatlike on the precipice;

Hand that eager in its motion
Moved to the unselfish act—

All that fine articulation
Now is quite another fact.
What supplants your former being
Claiming for itself your name,
Like a wave forever fleeing
Came, and passes, just the same.

Let the end and the beginning
Merge themselves, then, into one!
Swifter than the time-world's spinning
Fly, for flying's never done.
Thank the muses for their lessons
Promising the unmarred whole:
In your heart the unchanged essence,
And the pure form in your soul.

1803

Night Song

Ah, from your pillowed dreaming,
Give me but half an ear!
Now, while my lute is thrumming,
Sleep on—what would you more?

Now, with my lute-song blending,
The starry legions pour
Blessings on love unending;
Sleep on—what would you more?

This breath of love unending
Lifts me now high and clear
From earth's tumultuous grinding:
Sleep on—what would you more?

On earth's tumultuous straining
Too well you'd shut my door;
I'm banished, chill, complaining—
Sleep on—what would you more?

I'm banished, chill, unblooming,
But in your dream, give ear:
Might I thy pillowed dreaming
Sleep too—what would you more?

1804

The Sonnet

To practice a revived artistic kind
Is an expected, holy obligation:
You too may follow the prescribed dictation,
As step by step it regulates your mind.

For what you loved was how the form confined
In limits the wild spirits' agitation;
However violent their inclination,
The work would find its shaped and proper end.

So I'd in artful sonnets like to fettle
With rhyme and measure eloquent and limber
Whatever my emotion gave to do;

For this, though, I can't comfortably settle,
Loving to hew things from a single timber,
And otherwise would sometimes have to glue.

1806

The Metamorphosis of the Animals

If you have dared prepare yourself to ascend the last ledges
Up to the summit, then give me your hand and open your eyes to
Freely gaze on the white and blemishless field of Nature.
Goddess, she spends the rich gifts of life ungrudging about her,
Feels, though, none of the mortal mother's concern for her
    children's
Nurture and care, for it not beseems her; she lays down a higher
Law that is twofold, establishing bounds to every life form,
Giving it limited needs, but giving, too, gifts unlimited;
Easy to find, she scatters them forth, and gently favors
Most the vigorous toil of her so often needy children
Wantonly swarming out in urgent pursuit of their calling.

Every beast is an end in itself, full-formed it issues
Forth from the lap of Nature, and in turn begets fully formed
    offspring.
Every organ develops according to laws eternal,
Even the rarest form preserving, strangely, the archetype.
Every mouth, then, is deft to grasp and engage the provender
Best befitting the body; be the jaw weak and toothless,
Be it mightily toothed, in every case whatever
Aptly a suitable organ conveys to the limbs their nutrition.
Likewise every foot, whether long or short, will function
Quite in harmony, fitting the animal's needs and senses.

So for all her offspring the fullest and purest well-being
Stems from the mother; living members never stand in
Contradiction; all of them work for life together.
Thus the form of the animal drives its habit of living,

Function, though, strongly shaping in turn the form that defines it.
So it makes manifest all of its ordered unfolding emergence,
Which, in its changing bent, is shaped by external beings.
Still, it's within that the power of the nobler animals finds itself,
Bounded inside the holy cycle of living development,
Bonds that no god can extend, since Nature honors their limits:
Only constrained in this way has perfection ever been possible.

Yet, from within, a spirit appears to violently struggle,
Seeking to break through the circle, create anew those structures,
Shaping the will; yet what it begins it begins without issue.
Though it may thrust itself into these given limbs or those others,
Fitting them mightily out, already another grows stunted;
Disproportionate burden destroys all beauty of structure,
Marring the form, negating its elegant cleanness of motion.
If then you see one animal blessed with some special advantage,
Ask yourself at once what deficiencies might it then suffer,
Somewhere else in its nature: search with inquiring spirit;
Soon you will find the key to all creative emergence.

Yes, for no animal ever can carry a horn on its forehead
When it has teeth that hedge the rim of its upper jawbone,
For the eternal Mother, let her bend all of her efforts,
Finds it impossible quite to fashion horns on a lion,
Lacking matter enough to plant a row of dentition
And at the same time sprout a setting of horns or antlers.

Take then in this noble conception of power and constraint, of
Whimsical choosing and law, of freedom and measure, motion
Acting in order, lack and advantage; the Muse so sacred
Bears it in harmony in on you, instructing with gentle
    compulsion.

No higher concept than this does the moral philosopher master,
Nor does the man of action, nor the poetic artist,
Only through it does the ruler rightly deserve his scepter.
Joy, you highest of Nature's creations, to know yourself equal
Thus to rethink her loftiest thought, to which she in her genius
Rose at the outset. Pause now, stand and turn your gaze backward,
Think, compare, and take from the lips of the Muse that now you
See, not only dream, the fullness of truth in its beauty.

1806

Farewell

A thousand kisses still though I was craving,
But one remained before our separation,
And parting's bitter-rooted pain and passion
Must be the shore I tear myself in leaving.

Rich pleasure yet there was in the perceiving
Of mountain, cot, and river, hill and ocean;
At length a pasture for the eyes, a blue gradation
Remained in the bright gloom of fleeing evening.

Last, as the sea's sill margined off my gazing,
Back to my heart my hot desire fell broken,
And vexed I sought what I had lost and wasted—

But lo, as if the sky at once was blazing,
It seemed that nothing had been lost or taken,
And I had everything I'd ever tasted.

1807

The Lover Writes Again

Why then once more to paper am I bending?
Do not, beloved, ask so critically:
I've naught to say—I mean it, actually—
But here it is: in your dear hand it's ending.

Because I cannot come, then what I'm sending
Should my whole heart to you unparted carry,
With joys, hopes, pleasures, pains sealed up entirely,
All which have no beginning and no ending.

From now on I can't trust you to construe
How with its sense, desire, its fancy, will,
My true heart is conveyed to you this way;

As once I stood before you, gazed at you,
My whole being full, no place to further fill,
And could say nothing; what then should I say?

1807–8

Eight Poems from *The West-East Divan, 1814–15*

Talismans

God's own is the Orient!
God's own is the Occident!
Northern lands and southern lands
Rest in peace within his hands.

He, the only righteousness,
Wills to all that righteousness;
By his hundred names may he
On high, Amen, all-praisèd be.

Error would my steps betray:
You know how to clear my way.
When I act and when I write,
Grant that my way be the right.

What though I'd seek an earthly prize,
That very thought adds to a higher prize—
Not to reduce the spirit down to dust,
For dust itself contains an upward thrust.

In every breath there are two kinds of grace:
Inhale, exhale, taking and giving place;
The former presses, the latter refreshes,
Life is a marvelous mixture of meshes.
Thank God when he oppresses you
And when he frees you, thank him too.

1814–15

Blessed Yearning

Do not tell the mocking nation,
Secrets only for the wise:
Life that longs for consummation
In the flames—that's what I'd praise.

In the night of love still cooling,
Where what made you, you were making,
You are wrought by a strange feeling
In the candlelight's soft shaking.

Now no more the darkness keeps you
Clasped in shadows meditating:
And a new desire now sweeps you
Upward to a higher mating.

Space can't clog your spellbound yearning,
You come flying just the same,
And at last, drawn to the burning,
You're the moth come to the flame.

You would be Earth's sullen guest
In the darkness glooming,
If you'd never felt this quest:
Die into becoming!

1814–15

To Zuleika

That with perfume's sweet caressing
You might heighten pleasure's lure,
First a thousand rosebuds, pressing,
Must their crucible endure.

If within this vial linger
Sweet eternal and unspoiled,
Be it slim as is your finger,
It would need a whole wide world:

Yes, a world of life and yearning,
Which in its full-blooded urge,
Sought the bulbul's lovesick burning,
And its soul-transforming dirge.

Say we're racked too by the heady
Pain that multiplies sought joy?
Did not Timur's rule already
Many million souls destroy?

1814–15

Ginkgo Biloba

This tree leaf, of the East's bestowing
Upon my garden, gives a clue
Or secret sense about its growing
A scientist may thus pursue:

Is it one single living being
That parts itself as it is done?
Or are they two that by agreeing
May then be known as only one?

To this deep question I, replying,
Surely discovered what was true:
Don't you too find my songs implying
That I am one but also two?

1814–15

Limitless

(To Hafiz)

You cannot end—that is what makes you great,
Nor did you ever start—that is your fate.
Your song turns like the starry vault transcending,
Always the same in onset and in ending,
And what the middle brings is simply that
With which it ended, where it started at.

The true poetic spring of every pleasure,
You flow out, wave on wave, beyond all measure;
Lips ready always for a tender kiss,
A heartsong rushing sweetly from its giver,
A throat all fiery for a drink of bliss,
A noble breast that pours itself forever.

Then let the whole world sink and founder!
Hafiz, with you, with you alone
I would contend! Pleasure and pain,
Twins, we have ever shared as one!
In pride, I'll live my life the sounder
To love and drink as you have done.

Now sound with your own fire, my song!
You are more ancient, and more young.

1814–15

In a Thousand Forms

Though in a thousand forms you may conceal you,
Yet, All-belovèd, soon I know it's you;
Whatever veils of magic-weaving seal you,
All-presence, still I know it's you.

In the young cypresses, their pure limbs glowing,
All-shapeliest, I know at once it's you;
In the canal's pure life-wave softly flowing,
You All-caressing, well I know it's you.

When the tall fountain climbs in its unfolding,
All-playful, I rejoice that it is you;
When the clouds change, all molding and unmolding,
All-manifold, I find that it is you.

In the embroidered veil of meadow flowers
All-tint-bestarred in beauty, it is you;
And thousand-armed the clinging ivy bowers
All-clasping, tell me always that it's you.

And when the sunrise kindles in the ridges,
I greet the dawn, All-halcyon, as you;
And then pure heaven with its arching bridges
All-heart-enlarging, breathes the breath of you.

What I with outward sense and inward knowing
Perceive, All-teacher, that I do through you;
And naming Allah's hundred names onflowing,
Each one is echoed by a name for you.

1814–15

The Higher and the Highest

Teaching this should be unbounded,
We must not be punished for it;
That it all might be expounded,
Let your deepest quest explore it:

So you'll grasp how human being
Finds a way that we can love us,
Eagerly a true home seeing,
Both beneath us and above us.

And, my darling, I admit it:
I would want the old known pleasures,
Ease I've relished, to me fitted,
In Hereafter's higher measures.

So I joy in gardens, bowers,
All we here below found pleasant,
Pretty children, fruit, and flowers:
Old souls, too, rejuvenescent.

So I'm yearning now to gather
All my young and old friends hither,
In the German tongue to stammer
Paradise's own palaver—

Men's and angels' strange inflection
In their mutual caresses,
Grammar of that mute declension,
Both the poppy's and the rose's.

*

One is happiest when in glances
One the rhetoric of love expresses,
Heavenly sweetness thus advances
In those voiceless silentnesses.

Tone and sound find liberation
From the word's confined immanence:
The Enlightened One's sensation
Of a limitless transcendence.

So, in Paradise the senses
Must persist in that aliveness:
Feeling now without the fences,
One sense in exchange for fiveness.

And so thus I pierce all places,
Lightly through the spheres eternal,
By the word's vibrating traces,
That are God's melodic kernel.

Freed from hot desire's binding,
No end lets itself be captured;
Face to face with love unending,
Through the air we drift enraptured.

1818

Elements

Say, what elements must nourish
Every true song for its growing?
That the layman feel its flourish,
Master, hear its joy-bestowing?

Love's our theme above all others
When we sing, its celebrating;
Song drinks in the love of lovers
Permeating, resonating.

There must be the clink of glasses,
Ruby wine-glow winking witty,
So for lovers as for drinkers,
Poems be garlands sweet and pretty.

And the sound of weapons clashing,
And the crash of trumpets glorious,
So when joy flames up, besieging
Hero turns to god victorious.

For the poet hates what's ugly:
It's the poet's bounden duty,
What's misshapen and unlovely
He will not let live as beauty.

Those four ancient stuffs the singer
Knows to mix with force and rigor:
To the people he's the bringer,
Like Hafiz, of joy and vigor.

before 1815

from *Parabolic*

A poem is a painted windowpane!
From the market look into the chapel:
A gloomy and a dark confine.
It seems that way to Mr. Philistine:
Well might he be a bitter apple
And bitter all his life remain.

But just suppose he came inside,
Greeted the holy little shrine
Now colored with such light divine:
Story and ornament both shine,
Meaning and parable allied,
And fit for you, God's children, to
Rejoice your eyes and be made new!

1815

Limitation

I know not what I find so dear
In this small world so cramped and near,
What sweet enchantment binds me here;
For I forget, gladly forget
How strange that destiny should call me;
And ah! What things prepared and set
I feel within that must befall me.
O might it be that my right lot be found!
What's still wrapped up for me must be
Fulfilled by sweet vitality,
A present silence, future hope—to be unbound!

1815

To Luna

Sister of the primal light,
Image of a tender grieving!
Mists float silver, rain-bright, laving
Your sweet face across the night;
And your footsteps, soft and light,
From the caves of day's confining
Wake the lost souls, sad and pining,
Me, and all the birds of night.

How your searching glance surveys
That expanse, so vast and empty;
Lift me up beside you, grant me!
Grant my rapture what it prays,
That in a voluptuous peace
This sly cavalier may witness
Through the glass of his girl's lattice
Her night's sweet unconsciousness.

That dear happiness of sight
Soothes the pains of separation,
And I glean your radiation,
And I hone my gazing bright;
Lighter now the light is shone
Round her pretty unclothed members;
Now she draws me to her slumbers
As you, by Endymion.

1815

Lovely Is the Night

Now I leave her modest dwelling,
My beloved's quiet abode,
And with secret step I'm stealing
Through the desolate dark wood.
Luna breaks through oaks and bushes,
Zephyr intimates she's near;
And the pungent bowing birches
Strew for her sweet incense here.

How I joy in this soft coolness
Of the lovely summer night!
Oh, how silent is this stillness
Of the inner soul's delight!
Scarcely may we grasp the pleasure,
Yet, O heaven, I would part
With a thousand such nights' treasure
For just one with my sweetheart.

1815

Muteness

When the loved one with her lover
Trades for his a stolen look,
Then in verse the poet ever
Sings the joy of such good luck;
Muteness, though, brings greater fullness,
Purchasing a richer trust;
Silence, silence! Stillness, stillness!
That's the luck that is the best.

When the warrior, fierce with clamor
Of the trumpet and the drum,
Smites the naked foe, a hammer
Hurling them from whence they come;
Victory deserving reverence,
He accepts his fame's applause,
But it is a secret reverence
That is truly virtue's cause.

Hail to us! We band of brothers
Know what no one else can hear;
Yes, those songs well-known to others
Sheathe themselves within our sphere.
No one should, nor will he, witness
What to each other we commit;
For it is on faithful muteness
That the temple walls are set.

1816

Proem

In whose name, who alone is self-created!
Of His own calling, self-originated;
In whose name, who makes faith and trust to be,
Love, and the power of action, energy;
In whose name, He who is so often named,
Whose essence is unknown, however claimed.

In what the ear, in what the eye can seize,
You know Him only by such similes;
And where your spirit's highest fire-flight shines,
It is fulfilled with likenesses and signs.
You're drawn, you're swept so joyfully away,
Beauty invests your wanderings, your way.
You count no more, you reckon not the time:
Your quest's each step is measureless, sublime.

·

What God is He, who all the world transcends,
Letting the All spin through His fingers' ends!—
Yet from within to move the world sees fit,
Sees nature in Himself, and Him in it,
So what in Him lives, weaves, and is, keeps still
His power, his spirit, and creative will.

·

Within things' inmost, too, a whole world plays,
And thus the people's custom we should praise,

That whatsoever is the best he's known
He names his God, his very own;
Grants Him the earth and heaven above,
His fear—when possible, his love.

1816

Ur-Words: Orphic

1. *Daimon:* Daemon

As on the day that lent you to Creation,
The Sun stood up to meet the planets' greeting,
You waxed and throve within the dispensation
Of that great Law you served in its completing;
So must you be, you brook no self-evasion,
So said the sibyls, prophets so repeating;
Nor time nor force can shatter the resolving
Of that stamped form, its vital self-evolving.

2. *Tyche:* Chance

A wanderer, within us and outside us,
Happily skirts those strictest limitations;
We're not alone; we grow where others guide us,
Doing as others do on such occasions;
Chance in our lives can help or override us,
A toy that plays through us in its mutations.
So soon the cycling years have gently dwindled:
The lamp awaits the flame to be enkindled.

3. *Eros:* Love

Inevitable! Down from heaven falling,
Where once from ancient chaos he ascended,
But here he flits on airy wings excelling,
In heart and mind to make a spring day splendid,
He seems to flee, by fleeing still recalling,
Turns grief to joy, the tremblings sweetly ended.
Some hearts are only drawn to the ideal:
The noblest gives itself to one, the real.

4. *Ananke:* Necessity
Again, as the stars will, so it is fated:
Law and constraint—and will is but desiring
What we can't help but want, predestinated,
And choice is silent in the will's requiring,
And all that's dearest flees as if it's hated,
And the hard "Must" commands our art's aspiring.
Then all these years we saw as freedom-winning
Leave us more trapped than in the first beginning.

5. *Elpis:* Hope
Such brazen walls, such bonds of vile constraining,
Such gates may be unlocked yet, though they're founded
On rock and stone, their ancient rule sustaining.
A being parts them, weightless and unbounded,
From mist, from cloud, from shadows sweetly raining,
She wings us, lifts us up, free and ungrounded.
You know her well, in all climes she may waken;
One wingbeat!—and the aeons overtaken!

1817–18

At Midnight

At midnight I would go—not of my choosing—
A tiny boy, down to the Father's house,
And in the graveyard, star on star was blazing,
And one and all shone lovely, glorious
   In that midnight.

Later on I, in life's enlarging circle,
Must needs go to my love, she drew me so;
The stars and the aurora in high battle,
I breathed in, there and back, a blissful glow
   In that midnight.

Till finally the full moon's luminescence
Clearly and plainly thrust into my gloom,
And thought, too, sensual in its willing essence,
Snaked quickly round what's past and what's to come,
   In that midnight.

1818

Refinding

Star of stars, do I now truly
Press you to my heart again?
What dark night, unsounded valley,
Lengthens separation's pain!
You are to my every pleasure
Sweet beloved counterpart;
Even now I quake, to measure
That past ache, that bitter smart.

When the world in its deep founding
Lay on God's eternal breast,
He with shaping joy unbounding
Formed the first hour of the rest:
Let it be! the Word he uttered,
Called forth then an anguished "Ah!"
And with this great thrust now shattered,
All became all things that are.

Light then *did* itself! It parted
Its shy eclipse from what it is;
Now the atoms, bifurcated,
Fled each other's genesis.
Swiftly seeking what was placeless,
Each strove outward into space;
Numb, in the unmeasured wasteness,
Soundless, lustless, passionless.

All was silent, dumb, vacated:
God now first felt loneliness!

Rosy dawn he then created,
Pity wrung from raw distress;
Now the colors, light occluded,
Started their harmonic play,
And what fell when it exploded,
Loved again what went astray.

So what should belong together
Strives to seek each other's lack,
And to life, unmeasured ever,
Feeling, looking, now came back.
Be it seized, and for the taking,
If it only grasp and hold!—
Allah now may cease his making,
We will now create his world.

So with rosy daybreak pinions,
I am raptured to your lip,
And the seals of night, in millions,
Bond our starlit partnership.
Here we are, on Earth together,
Exemplars of joy and pain;
Let another "Fiat!" never
Separate us once again.

1819

In Honor of Luke Howard

When the high godhead Kamarupa flies
Swaying in mass and lightness, roams the skies,
Gathers the air-veil's foldings, strews them forth,
Joys in the change of forms above the earth,
Now he stands fixed, now vanishes like dreams,
Amazed, we doubt our eyes, what is or seems;

Now boldly stirs his power to simulate,
That shapes the vague and the determinate;
There threats a lion, there heaves an elephant,
A camel's neck becomes a dragon's front;
An army marches up but dips its flag,
Its power broken on a lofty crag;
The loyalest of all cloud-couriers lost,
Undone before he finds the far loved post.

But Howard gives us with his mind's clear eyes
A new-forged teaching, heaven's highest prize.
What was ungraspable, he touches, holds;
Defines the vague, determines and unfolds,
Hits on the proper name—be honor yours!
(How this strange cloud-streak rises, rears,
Balls itself in a mass, dissolves unfurled.)
You are remembered by a grateful world.

Stratus
When from the water-mirror's plain of night
Fog's level carpet rises, still and white,

The moon blends with this surging glimmer-show,
A ghost engendering more ghosts below.
Then are we all, O Nature, we concede,
But children, happy innocents indeed!
Now rises on the mountain layer on layer
Accumulating in the far dark air,
Equally liable to fall as dew
Or rise into the air-world's midnight blue.

Cumulus
And if then in the higher atmosphere
The eager stuff be called on to appear,
The tall cloud fists itself in splendor higher,
Broadcasting, building up its work of power,
That you both fear and then, by feeling, know:
It threatens from above, and shakes below.

Cirrus
Higher, yet higher, rears the noble surge!
Redemption's weightless, a celestial urge.
In flakes dissolves the heaped-up primal stock,
Like pattering sheep combed lightly to a flock.
So what was born so easily below
Last to the Father's lap and hand will flow.

Nimbus
Now let what has conglobed below be drawn
By the earth's stark gravity strongly down,
Have itself out in raging weather-thunder,

Roll through in pawing hosts and blow asunder!—
To suffer as to do, Earth's destiny!
Yet by this image, raise your eyes and see:
Speech reaches down, the better to express,
Spirit seeks upward still, for changelessness.

1820

Always and Everywhere

Pierce the mountain's deepest vaulting,
Chase the clouds to heaven exalting,
Muse cries out to brook and valley
Thousandfold, continually.

When a fresh calyx blooms, that day
   It calls for a new sonnet;
And when time, rushing, flees away,
   Seasons return upon it.

1820

The One and the All

In boundlessness to find one's being,
Gladly from selfhood selfhood freeing,
There all vexations are unbent,
All hot desires and wild temptations,
All dull demands and obligations,
Lost in a sweet relinquishment.

World-soul, come pierce us! As its vessel
Then with its Spirit let us wrestle,
Our highest challenge thus obeyed.
Let virtuous genii then guide us,
Our noblest masters, lightly lead us
To Him who all things makes, and made.

And thus to re-create Creation,
Not armed in paralyzed fixation,
The living Act works ever on.
And what was not, is now becoming,
Pure suns and painted earths still blooming,
Unresting where it once has gone.

It will drive on, shaping, disclosing
All form itself, then decomposing;
Time but pretends to still persist.
In all, the Eternal's the unfolder,
Thus all to nothingness must molder
So it continue to exist.

1821

Trilogy of Passion

To Werther

Once more you dare, you much-lamented shadow,
To venture out into the day's clear light,
Meet me afresh in that wild-flowered meadow
And do not, as you well might, shun my sight.
It is as if you dwell in time's first dawning,
Where we are quickened by the fields' bright haze,
And after day's travail and long heart-burning
We feel with joy the sun's last parting rays.
To stay was my fate; yours was just to go.
You went ahead—and didn't miss much, though.

The life of man seems such a splendid plight:
The day how lovely, and how grand the night!
Planted in Eden's sweet felicity,
The glorious sun no sooner do we see
But we are tangled in the bitter strife
Both with ourselves and with our place in life;
With neither is the other satisfied,
The outside darkens, while it glows inside,
A bright face hides the dark glance that denies it,
We're lucky—but we do not recognize it.

Now we believe we do! With violent force
A girlish sweetness draws us to its source:
As happy as his boyhood flowering
In spring the swain steps forth as he were spring,
Shocked with the honey—who has wrought this bliss?—
He looks around, the whole wide world is his.

Into that world, unbound by court or wall,
His haste compels him to explore it all;
And as a bird-flock skims about a tree,
So swarms he in the steps of his fair she;
He would fain leave the free air of his past,
And seeks the true glance that will bind him fast.

Yet, warned too early and again too late,
He finds his flight hemmed in, the snare's fair bait,
Reunion is a joy, to part is pain;
The re-reunion sweeter yet again;
Years are repaid in one blink of an eye,
Yet lies in wait the treacherous goodbye.

My friend, you smile with feeling, as is fit;
You parted horribly, are famed for it;
We celebrated your ill-luck, and so
You left us on our own to weal or woe;
Then we were dragged once more down that dark way
Into the labyrinths of passion's sway;
Tangled in needs, the needs we're tangled by
Lead us to parting—and to part's goodbye!
How we are moved then when the poet sings
To stay the death that separation brings!
Half-guilty, tangled in pain's ligatures,
A god gives him to say what he endures.

Elegy

And so when mortals in their pain are dumb,
God gave me how to speak of what I suffer.
What should I hope for from another meeting,

From this shut blossom, closed so many a day?
Paradise, hell, stand wide to your entreating;
Your mood so wanders on its errant way!—
No doubt now! See, she steps toward heaven's gate,
Arms out to raise you into your sweet fate.

So were you then in paradise unwaning
Received as worthy of eternal blisses,
No wish remained in you, no hope, no pining,
The quest at end, no dearer goal than this is,
And contemplation of this beauty burning
Dried up the sources of those tears of yearning.

How the day there stirred not its soft-fledged pinion!
How did the minutes heap before its driving!
The evening kiss a binding seal of union,
Through the next sunrise fresher still surviving.
The wandering hours, like sisters seen together
Seemed all the same, yet none just like the other.

That last kiss cuts to shreds, with gruesome sweetness,
A marvelous soft mesh of love and lack.
The foot trips at the gate in all its fleetness
As if a flaming cherub turned it back.
The eye stares dully at its dark path, but
When it looks back the gate's already shut.

And now this heart is shut as that is, even
As it had never opened, as if hours
Of bliss with her, where every star of heaven
Blazed in vain rivalry, were never ours;
And gloom, remorse, and blame, the weight of trouble,
In this oppressive air now bend it double.

Then is there of this world nothing remaining?—
The cliffs no longer crowned with holy shadows?
No harvest ripening toward its graining?
With bloom and bush, no green-spread river-meadows?
Domes not that supermundane grandeur high beyond,
Now rich in form, now wantonly unformed?

How light and graceful, clear and finely woven
Floats seraph-like in the blue fragrant ether
A slender image of her high in heaven
Borne from a choir of earnest clouds beneath her:
And so you saw her lead into the dancing
Of all entrancing forms, the most entrancing.

Only for moments may you try to capture
Instead of her an image air-begotten;
Back to the heart—there you best find that rapture,
Where she in changing forms stirs unforgotten;
So thus the One in Many shapes its being
A thousand times more lovely in the seeing.

How graciously she waited at her door
And still thereafter blessed me in my steps;
After the last kiss, even swept me to her
And pressed the very last one on my lips:
So clear and moving still my true love's picture
Burns in this constant heart as fiery scripture.

That heart, as steadfast as high battlements,
The keep that keeps her, and that she keeps in her,
Rejoicing in its changeless permanence,
Knowing when she reveals what is within her,

Feels freest in those bounds she loves so dearly,
And beats for thankfulness, and for that merely.

Was the ability to love, was needing,
Quenched by a counter-love, annihilated?
And can that lust for hope, joy, making, seeding,
Choosing, swiftly doing, be soon created?
If love possessed a lover's spirit ever,
It did so loveliest with this poor lover,

Indeed through her!—A qualm of deep unease
Presses on soul and flesh its drear duress,
The gaze is ringed with shuddery images
In this void space, choking heart-emptiness;
Still hope once more, from this known threshold, dawns
And she appears, in a mild radiance.

The peace of God that passeth understanding—
So it is written—do I now compare
To that so joyful sense of peace attending
The presence of the creature we adore;
There rests the heart and nothing alien stirs
That deepest feeling, that your soul is hers.

In our hearts' purity beats a desire
Grateful, and free, and innocently shameless,
To give ourselves to something purer, higher,
Unveiled before the eternal and the nameless;
We call it piety!—that exalted place
I feel I share, standing before her face.

Before her gaze, as in the sun's bright power,
Before her breath, as in the spring's warm breezes,

Now melts the self-sense, fixed through year and hour
In winter's ice-caves where the spirit freezes;
Before her coming, as the ice is shattered,
All will and interest of self are scattered.

It is as if she said "Each moment we
Are given life in friendship as we grow.
Yesterday gave us little novelty,
Tomorrow is forbidden us to know,
And if I feared the coming of the night
The sinking sun still gazed on my delight.

"Do then as I; in happy understanding
Look in the present's eyes! Be swift in seeing!
I greet it quick, alive and undemanding;
Only for act, for joy, does love have being.
All is where you are only; like a child
You are invincible, you are the world."

Well said, I thought—surely some god supplied
This moment's grace to be your chaperone;
And who would not be on your lovely side,
Whom, as her darling now, fate makes her own?
I dread what parts me from you, you can see;
Such lofty wisdom—ah, what boots it me!

Now am I parted far indeed! What should
Behoove me now to do? I cannot say;
She offers me in beauty something good
That only burdens, I would throw away;
I'm driven about by a resistless yearning,
And endless tears are now the only learning.

Let them spurt forth, then! and flow unabated;
Yet never can they quench the inner burning!
It rips and sears my breast now, never sated,
Death strives with life in gruesome table-turning;
Though salves exist to still the body's grief,
The spirit lacks the will to seek relief.

Fails in concept—how could it go astray?
A thousand times it iterates her vision
That lingers now, and now is torn away,
Now indistinct, now lit with pure precision;
But how could this small comfort serve, deceiving,
This ebb and flow, when coming is but leaving?

And you, my true companions, leave me too!
Leave me alone in rock and moss and moor;
Onward! The world still opens wide to you,
The earth is vast, heaven great and grand and pure;
Seek Nature, she who takes in everything,
Her stammered secrets now deciphering.

All's all I have, my self's self-dispossessed—
Self once the darling of the gods, who lent
Pandora to me, put me to the test,
So rich in good, more in imperilment;
They blessed my lips with gifts, urged me to this,
They picked me out, plunged me in the abyss.

Reconciliation

Passion brings pain!—and who can recompense
The choked heart for its endless loss and pain?
And whither fled those hours so swiftly hence?
The loveliest was picked for you in vain!
The spirit clouds, its birth is tangled quite,
The great world vanishes from sense and sight!

Now floats out angel-music, wave on wave,
Tone upon tone inwoven, million-glowing,
The human essence to enpierce and lave
With an eternal beauty overflowing:
The eyes are wet with yearning, feel no less
The music's god-gifts than the tears they bless.

And so the eased heart notes in tremblingness
That it still beats and chooses to be beating,
In pure thanks for the present's rich largesse,
Its offer of itself ever repeating.
Just then it felt—O moment, ever stay!—
Love, and that music, twofold in sweet play.

1823–24

The Pariah

Mighty Brahma, lord of powers!
All things issue from Thy semen,
So from whom all justice flowers!
Did you only make the Brahmin,
Kshatriya, and merchant peer,
Were they only from thy shaping,
Or did you permit an apeling,
To become no less than we are?

Nobleness—we cannot claim it:
Wickedness is ours, a dying
—That dark word that others name it—
Is our species' multiplying.
This though true for our despisers
Should by you be held unholy:
That you can upbraid us, truly
All the greater should you prize us.

Hearing, Lord, my lowly prayer,
Bless me, as your child so find me,
Or let something come to flower
That to you would ever bind me!
For you've raised a very goddess
From among the temple dancers,
And we, praising such your answers,
This great wonder joy to witness.

probably 1823

The Bridegroom

At midnight as I slept my heart, delighted,
Woke love-filled as it were already day;
The day appeared to me as if benighted—
Why does this mean so much to me, I say.

I missed her, yes; my busy up and doing
I bore alone for her through hour and heat;
But then how life revived itself, renewing,
On that cool evening! it was good and meet.

The sun set then, and hand in hand enplighted,
We greeted then her last warm blessing glance,
And eyes to eyes spoke frankly and united:
Hope to the east, for her returning thence.

I'm led at midnight by the stars' white glitter
In sweet dream to the threshold of her rest.
O rest be granted me too, in that quarter!
Whatever else it be, our life is blessed.

probably 1825

A Better Understanding (from *The West-East Divan*)

He who poetry would know
Into poem-land must go;
He who would the poets know
Into poet-land must go.

So the West, as does the East,
Offers something pure to taste;
Shun the fancy, leave the waste,
Sit down to a splendid feast:
Not a moment should you wish
Disdain upon this glorious dish.

He who knows both self and other,
Here must grant acknowledgement:
No more can we part or sever
Orient and Occident.

So between two worlds, I grant it,
One may oscillate and swing,
Eastward, westward, fly enchanted—
That would be the finest thing!

Crossing Erfurt lately, I,
Who there oft perambulated,
Found that as in years gone by
I was warmly tolerated:

When the old folk give me greeting
From their humble homes, together,

Youth then seems to be repeating,
Which we'd sweetened for each other—

This one was the baker's daughter,
Next to her, the cobbler-girl;
No owl the third, but something hotter;
That one made of life a whirl.

So our effort is incessant
To surpass Hafiz at last:
To be happy in the present,
And take pleasure in the past.

probably 1826

from *The Legacy*

Nothing that truly is can perish!
All feel the Eternal's power to cherish:
Hold yourself blest in Being's embrace.
Being's eternal; for its measures
Safeguard the precious living treasures
With which the All adorns its grace.

Truth was found long since; its dominion
Bound the high spirit in communion:
That old truth, always hold it fast!
Son of the earth, thank that wise Reason
Who showed her how the sun, in season,
Turns, and turns all her kin at last!

Turn inward now at once, discover
Your center in yourself forever—
That noble mind cannot deny.
You shalt not lack for rule or border
Because the conscience, its own order,
In Morals' day is sun in sky.

You must on sense be then relying,
That shows the nothing that is lying,
If waking intellect's unfurled.
See freshly then, and happy surely,
And wander lightly and securely
The prairies of the gifted world.

In compass taste its ample blessing:
Reason should rule in all assessing,

Where life is life's felicity.
Thus what is past stands on its founding,
What is to come is life abounding,
The present is eternity.

And have you finally succeeded,
Are you by feeling pierced and seeded?
Only what's fruitful is what's true;
Put to the proof the world's prescriptions—
Its nature circumscribes its options—
Join yourself to the smallest crew.

Of old, in stillness dedicated,
Poet, philosopher created
A work of love self-willed, inspired;
Just so, make lovely grace your duty:
To prophesy the new soul's beauty,
Call deepliest to be desired.

1829

from *The Chinese-German Daybook-Yearbook*

Twilight from the heights . . .

Twilight from the heights descended,
All that once was near is far;
Now arise the sweet and splendid
Glitters of the evening star!
All sways into unknown darkness,
Mists steal slowly up the crests;
Shade now deepens into blackness,
Mirroring, the lake now rests.

And in those great eastern shadows
I surmise the moon-gleam's glow;
Willow tresses in the meadows
Play upon the streamlet's flow.
In their shadow-games, atremble
Luna's magic light takes part;
Through the eye creeps soft and nimble
Coolness calming to the heart.

1827–28

Full Moon Rising

Must your presence be so fleeting?
You were even now so near;
In the dark-massed clouds retreating,
Now you are no longer here.

Yet you feel how sorrow moves me,
Lo, your limb peeps out, a star!
Witness that my lady loves me,
Be my darling near or far.

Onward then! In candid splendor,
Brightening in your course of light;
Swift my heart beats sore and tender—
Over-blessèd is the night.

Dornburg, August 25, 1828

Dornburg

When at dawn hill, vale, and pleasance
Doff their veils of condensation,
And the buds with opalescence
Fill in yearning expectation;

When the ether, nimbus-bearing,
Strides on in the open skyway,
And the Easter wind, pursuing,
Gives the sun an azure highway;

If you thank, nursed by this vision,
The pure breast of Fair Excelling,
Then the sun's red valediction
Gilds the ringed horizon's dwelling.

1828

Ten Poems from *Faust*
1770–1829

1. Dedication
(To *Faust*, Part 1)

Come, you uncertain forms, who showed your features
So long ago to my dark-shadowed gaze,
Shall I now try to grasp you, fleeting creatures?
Does my heart seek that madness, those strange ways?
You draw me there! Work then, so please your natures,
Rising around me in your fume and haze.
As in my youthful days, my heart feels shaken
By that strong breath of magic you awaken.

You bring too, from past times, happier visions,
And some loved shadows rise up, calling me;
As in some lay from half-recalled traditions,
First come the scenes of love and amity,
Then pain renews, with anguished repetitions,
How wild and labyrinthine life can be,
And calls those dear ones who, fortune deceiving
Of their sweet hours, fell off and left me grieving.

They will not hear these notes, to whom they mattered,
The souls to whom I sang the first of them;
That friendly throng is parted now and scattered,
Faded, alas, that echo now is dumb!
An unknown crowd will hear the song that's uttered,
Applause only alarms my heart's loud drum.
Whoever else that found my verses stirring
If they still live, wander the world unhearing.

And I am seized by long-unwonted longing
For that serene and solemn realm of shades,
My halting song hovers with a vague ringing,
Like the Aeolian lyre in its glissades.
A shudder seizes me; tears, tears come stinging;
Now mild and weak, my strong heart's fury fades.
All I possess and am seems lost and banished,
And what's reality to me is what once vanished.

2. Prologue in Heaven

The three angels step forward.

RAPHAEL:
The sun joins as in ancient fashion
With brother-spheres' contesting song,
And its prescribed peregrination
Ends in a thunderclap more strong.
Its sight gives all the angels power,
But how, no being fathom may,
These works, ungrasped by any knower,
As splendid as in that first day.

GABRIEL:
Swift, swift, beyond the mind's grasp ranging,
The splendor of the earth rolls round,
The light of Paradise exchanging
With night's chill lightlessness profound.
The sea pours shining in its pother
From deep base up the cliff's steep waste,
And cliff and sea are torn together
Along the spheres' eternal haste.

MICHAEL:
And storms rage, each with each competing,
From sea to land, from land to sea,
A furious chain of cause creating,
Across the world's immensity.
There flames the lightning's devastation,
Before the thunderbolt's pathways;
Yet, Lord, thy heralds' veneration
Is for thy gentler turning days.

ALL THREE:
This sight gives all the angels power,
But how, no being fathom may,
And all thy works, in their high flower,
Are splendid, as in that first day.

3. Faust in His Study

I've studied—ach—philosophy,
Medicine, law, and, more's the pity,
Consuming endless energy,
The wasteland of theology;
And stand here, foolish sophomore,
No wiser than I was before!
They call me Master, even Doctor now,
And round and round, I know not how,
For ten long useless years I chose
To lead my students by the nose—
That's why my hot heart burns me so,
Because I know we cannot know.
Yes, I'm a smarter fool than those
Professors, scribes, and holy joes;
No doubts or scruples plague my cell,
I fear no Devil, nor his Hell—
But that's just why my joy is fled,
All my pretense of wisdom dead,
All pose of teacher but a sham;
No guide or counselor I am.
Nor have I either goods or gold,
My name's not honored or extolled,
No dog would want to live like me.
And so I've set my soul on sorcery,
To try whether the spirits' potency
Might not unveil the mysteries to me,
That I no longer, in a sweat of shame,
Name what I do not have the names to name,
That I may know what secret law or force
Unites the cosmos in its course,
And look into the seeds of life, and cease

To cram into mere words the universe.
O you full moon, once more again
Would that you might behold my pain
That many a midnight with its ache
Has kept me at this desk awake:
And over books and papers wise,
My friend so gloomy-souled, arise!
Ah, might I on the mountainside
Walk in your lovely light, and glide
With spirits over the crevasse
Or twilight meadow, floating, pass;
Unburdened of all knowing-pain,
Bathe in your dew, be whole again!

4. Faust Translating the Gospel

"In the beginning was the Word."
I'm stuck at once! Who'd help me if I erred?
I do not hold the word as such a treasure:
I must find then a different measure
If I would trust the spirit's influence.
"In the beginning"—write it then—"was Sense."
Ponder this first line and its leaning:
Don't let your pen outpace the meaning!
Is it then sense, the mind, that is the source?
"In the beginning," then, perhaps, "was Force."
But as I write I hear an admonition
That I not leave it with that definition.
The spirit moves me! I see it now, in fact:
Boldly write "In the beginning was the Act."

5. In Martha's Garden

MARGARETE:
. . . Do you believe in God?

FAUST: Love, who can say
"Yes, I believe in God"?
Ask the priest and wise man, and what they
Will answer sounds like mockery
Of her who asks the question.

MARGARETE:

                         So you don't believe?

FAUST:
Oh, sweet-faced innocent, don't misconceive!
Who can name Him,
Who can claim him,
Saying "I believe"?
Who presume
To say "I don't believe"?
The all-containing,
All-sustaining,
Does He not embrace, sustain
you, and myself, and Him?
Above, does not the sky arch high,
Below, the firm earth steadfast lie?
Do not the friendly stars eternal rise,
Do we not see each other, eyes in eyes?
And do not all things strive
Toward your head and heart,
And do not all things weave

Themselves with everlasting secrecy,
Seen thus unseen, into your closest intimacy?
        Fill up your heart with this,
And when your feelings overflow with bliss
Name it as you wish by any name whatever!
Luck, call it! Heart! Love! God!
I have no name to call it!
Feeling is all—
A name is but sound and smoke,
Clouding the glow of heaven.

MARGARETE:
This is all well and good.
It's what the priest says, more or less,
Except the words are rather different.

6. Mephistopheles Speaks

A dying nation leaves behind it
Only a shadow-bolt of gray:
You see it, but to grasp and bind it
You run in vain through night and day.

Whoever reaches after shades
Gets empty air for his endeavor:
Who heaps up shades on former shades
Sees himself trapped in night forever.

7. The Bailey

[A flower vase in a niche for an image of the Mater
Dolorosa. *Gretchen is putting in fresh flowers.]*

Ah, Mercy,
Grief-majesty,
Bend down your face to my plight!
    A fiery dart
Has pierced your heart:
Your Son dead in your sight.
    With such sad sighs
Your turn your eyes
To the Father above in his might.

Who knows
What gnawing throes
Have torn my body so?
    What has made my poor heart quiver,
Dreadful yearning, dreadful fever,
Only you alone can know!

Wheresover I may go,
It hurts, it hurts, it hurts, and oh,
My bosom is so full of woe!
    Wheresoever I'm alone,
I groan, I groan, I groan,
For my heart is broken so.

The pot beside my window
I watered with many a tear
This morning when I plucked for you

And brought these flowers here—
    Light shone within my chamber
In the new-risen sun
When from my bed in wretchedness
I rose, the day begun.

Help! Help! From shame and death's despite,
Bend down your face,
Ah, full of grace,
In pity for my plight!

8. Gretchen at the Spinning Wheel

My peace is fled,
My heart weighs sore;
It's lost forever,
Forevermore.

Where he is not
Is burial:
The whole wide world's but
Grave and gall.

My poor poor head
Has turned its wits,
My poor poor mind
Is all in bits.

My peace is fled,
My heart weighs sore;
It's lost forever,
Forevermore.

My window serves merely
His coming to see;
I leave the house only
His seeker to be.

His noble step,
His elegance,
His gentle smile,
His powerful glance—

*

And then his speech,
Its magic flow,
His hand's strong touch,
His kisses—oh—

My peace is fled,
My heart weighs sore;
It's lost forever,
Forevermore.

My bosom urges
Itself to his;
Ah, might I hold him,
Ah, might I kiss

Just as I wish it,
Just as I felt,
And with his kisses
I might melt!

9. Faust's Remorse

What's this within her arms, this heaven-sweetness?—
I'll warm myself on her breasts' whiteness:
Still, can't I feel her yearning grief?
And am I not the houseless, doomed to wander,
Unhuman, goalless, without peace,
Who roars, a waterfall, from cliff to cliff asunder,
Greedily raging after the abyss?
And she, the childlike innocent unwitting,
In her small alpine hut beside the fall,
Busied with homely chores befitting,
Her little world about her, all!
I had no satisfaction,
I, the God-abhorred,
But must to her destruction
Drag rock and house and board:
I must uproot her peace in this unfounding!
This offering, Hell, I burn at your demanding!
O Devil, may my time of dread not tarry—
Since it must be, then let it be!
Upon me fall her ruin when she miscarry,
And with her fate crush me!

10. Chorus Mysticus

All that is transient
Is but a fiction;
All insufficiency
Here becomes action;
All wordless mystery
Here may be done;
The ever-womanly
Still draws us on.

Natural Meanings: On Translation
Zsuzsanna Ozsváth & Frederick Turner

Poets notoriously struggle to write a poem. The poem does not present itself in the same words in which it finally appears; indeed, its fundamental appearance may be as much like a melody or a pattern of arabesques or colors or forces as like a pattern of words and syntax. Poets would not need to work if the English or French or Chinese sentences came straight to the mind of the American, French, or Chinese poet. Those words, even when after long rumination they pop into one's head, are already a crafted approximation of the mute original.

Current translation theory continues to accept the old supercilious joke about translation, that *traduire* is *trahir*, the *traduttore* is a *traditore*; the translator is a traitor. Poetry, said Frost, is what is lost in translation. But if every poem is *already* a translation, the poet's translation from the precursor ur-language in which the poet originally experienced the poem and the "fore-conceit" (as Sir Philip Sidney called it) of its meaning, then the whole picture changes. If another poet correctly receives the original poem in the ur-lan-guage, the translation of it in the translator-poet's native tongue may be just as accurate—possibly more!

We translators of this volume meet once or twice a week to translate together. German is a mother tongue for Ozsváth, a school subject for Turner. For both of us, Goethe is one of the supremely great poets of the world. To translate him together has been one of the most pleasurable things we have ever done. And, in breathing new life into Goethe's timeless writing, we have developed a marvelously collabo-rative practice.

Ozsváth first reads a passage of about ten to twenty lines in poetic German, paying attention to but not over-emphasizing the meter and rhyme. Turner comes to the passage without consulting a printed text in either language, so the experience is primarily oral. After a syllable and stress count, Turner recognizes the meter and creates a skeleton of the passage's meter and rhyme scheme. Then the words are translated by Ozsváth, in their various meanings and in the original order, and both translators then, if necessary, place them in correct English order. Turner inquires about the connotations, multiple meanings, normal context in use, class or occupational background, and historical usage of the words. Ozsváth notes whether the phrases are ordinary idiomatic German or whether Goethe is stretching the language or even making fun. She also adds relevant detail about the emotional force of the lines, their biographical or historical importance, and so on.

Turner writes down all this information in longhand, and the pair go on to the next passage. Often we break off to explore a puzzle or a contested interpretation, even moving on to larger philosophical, psychological, theological, or political implications, seeking to get into Goethe's mind as he composed. During the next few days Turner turns the result into dramatic poetry, being sure to preserve the same metrical form of the original, its rhyme pattern, its use of idiomatic or idiosyncratic usages, and its register—high style, low or middle, ironic, serious, playful, offensive, lyrical. Turner reads aloud the result at the beginning of our next meeting, and provides a paper copy of the text. Ozsváth critiques it for meaning, tone, and appropriateness, and Turner makes any needed corrections.

●   ●   ●

What has emerged from our long collaboration translating Hungarian and German poetry is a distinct perspective on the art of translation itself, which we find to be somewhat at odds with contemporary critical and literary theory, and may be of interest to the curious reader.

> Grau, theurer Freund, ist alle Theorie,
> Und grün des Lebens goldner Baum.[1]

> Look, my dear friend, all theory is gray,
> But green, green, is life's golden tree.

Mephistopheles' remark to the student he is corrupting in *Faust* could also be taken as Goethe's response to the great Dutch anatomist Petrus Camper, who had refused to accept Goethe's discovery of the human intermaxillary bone. What might this have to do with translation? Let us explain.

Camper was a distinguished supporter of the idea that humans were essentially different from apes. The issue went beyond the simple claim that we human beings had a special spiritual kinship with God that set us above the rest of the world. Each species of thing, as Aristotle had maintained, was a unique and eternal element in the universe. At the moment of creation, God created all the species of the world. The fact that species could be classified in a vast taxonomy simply indicated that God provided every animal and plant with the bodily structures and functions that it would require for its environment, and a taxonomic system is the most rational and elegant way of covering all the different conditions in the world. A hierarchy of categories can fill in the space between the universal and the particular. This is the "gray" theory that is contested by Faust and his mouthpiece Mephistopheles.

As an osteologist, Camper identified one feature in the human skeleton that marked its essential difference from that of the other animals: humans, he insisted, did not possess the intermaxillary bone, found in amphibians, reptiles, and mammals. This bone lies roughly in front of the skull at the tip of the upper jaw. Goethe, who was a serious scientist as well as a poet and philosopher, disproved Camper's theory by showing that human embryos *do* have a distinct inter-maxillary bone, which later in development becomes fused with the maxilla or palate but which can still be identified. Humans were not unique. Goethe wrote to Herder, an early evolutionist:

> I have found neither gold nor silver, but something that unspeakably delights me—the human Os intermaxillary! I was comparing human and animal skulls with Loder, hit up the right track, and behold—Eureka! Only, I beg of you, not a word—for this must be a great secret for the present. You ought to be very much delighted too, for it is like the keystone to anthropology—and it's there, no mistake! But how?[2]

Goethe's insight is that life is not a static taxonomic chart embodied in flesh and bone but a developmental process. The species are not discrete boxes in a taxonomic system but branches of a living tree. They change and evolve through their own striving (*Strebung*) for existence and a future, they generate and create themselves. And we are kin to all other living things, self-developing (*Bildung*), branching out new generations through sex, exploring new realms of being. So did our animal ancestors when they crawled onto the land, grew social brains, and started to change the environment rather than just adapt to it.

So Goethe's point about the green tree of life is to replace theory, in the sense of what is deemed logically nec-essary according to the definitions of words, with a living empirical fact: the baby's intermaxillary bone. As it gestates, this bone morphs into the front part of the palate with which the tongue makes our t's, d's, th's, and hissing s's.

It remained for Darwin to show the actual elegant mechanism of evolution, but the idea was already there in Goethe's time. Goethe knew the evolutionist Lamarck (whose work has recently been rehabilitated as a predecessor of epigenetics). In his remarkable poem "The Metamorphosis of the Plants," Goethe explicitly links the development of seed into plant with the evolution of the plant species itself and with the sexual drive that draws together Goethe and the beautiful listener to his poem. Every plant, Goethe said, is a variation of the *Urpflanze*, the archetypal plant from which they all derived. Animal species, too, had their own basic *Gestalt*, the four-leg, five-digit, spine-oriented form. And they too must have branched out from a shared ancestor.

• • •

What, to ask again, does this observation have to do with translation? Goethe was living in the heroic age of comparative philology, and the evident branching of the great tree of Indo-European languages was coming into shape. Goethe's own readings in the *Bhagavad Gita*, the Persian and Arabic poets, and Chinese novels and poetry had shown him that the people in them think, feel, and act just like "us" and that our many human languages might have their own *Urpflanze*, their own archetypal form or common ancestor. (Chomsky's generative grammar may be one later attempt at sketching its outline.) Goethe's *West-East Divan* is an explicit enactment of that idea; in his adaptations of Hafiz's poetry he "channels" Hafiz rather than merely painting him by numbers provided by the dictionary. And he can channel Hafiz because Hafiz is kin; his blood and the Persian's blood flowed in some shared mother's veins. The same applies to his *German-Chinese Daybook-Yearbook*.

Our own practice translating Hungarian poetry bore out the same discovery. In his translator's preface to a collection of Miklós Radnóti's poetry, Turner invoked the myth of Orpheus, who uses the power of the lyre and the song to enter the underworld and bring back his Eurydice from the dead:

Every poem is a flowering branch; to translate is to retrace the source of that branch's vitality down to where the other language branches off from the common root and to follow it up into a new bough or blossom. The tree of life is the tree of tongues; and under every poem's words is an ur-language in which it was spoken before the poet himself translated it into Magyar or Latin or English. The "original" has never been written down, and every poem is an approximation to that Orphic song which comes from the land of the dead, of the ever-living. Translation is not between leaf and leaf, flower and flower, but a descent through the fractal cascades of the twigs, the forked branches, to the root where the original poem issued from, and then, by the power of song, to reascend along another branch.

By the "ur-language" we do not mean some actual prehistoric language, like Indo-European. The ur-language is the deep language that we share to some extent with other higher animals, the language of childhood, the words we sometimes speak in dream and which dissolve when, having awoken, we try to remember them. The world itself speaks a sort of objective poetry, formed out of the harmonious relations of all registerings, sensations, and perceptions of it; and this poetry is the scaffolding of its next leap of growth. It is that poetry which poets hear, and which is the inner melody of their poems. The history of the evolution of perception and finally of aesthetic perception is the history of the evolution of the universe into concreteness and time, and into that densest and deepest kind of time we call eternity. The reason the rocks, trees, and beasts come to listen to Orpheus is because they want to hear how their own story comes out; for the ur-language that they speak is unconscious of itself and does not know its own meaning. The poet is the womb of that meaning, and needs the historical language of his or her culture to embody it.[3]

Given an adequate translator-poet, four requirements immediately present themselves if this perfect or better-than-perfect translation is to be possible.

First, that cultures and their languages are not "closed hermeneutic systems"—they are not incommensurable regimes of power and knowledge. That is, the foundation of much postmodernist theory must frankly be wrong. There is, in Goethe's words, a "keystone to the humanities," and it is our common evolutionary origin and our ancestral connection to the rest of nature. Only if we naively ignore the fact that all human cultures and languages derive from common ancestors—the essential principle of human evolutionary science, comparative linguistics, and human genetics—can we maintain that there is nothing in common between different human "constructions" of the world.[4]

Translation in the Goethean sense to which we subscribe presupposes that, however bizarrely different the expressions and connections of the source language are from those of the target language, they have common roots in human nature: in the "ur-language" we partly share with other mammals. Once we have identified and experienced that common root in the experience of the original writer, accurate translation should be possible. With demonstrably related languages, like German and English, that common root may indeed be identifiable through a root in the linguistic sense, a Germanic or Proto-Indo-European word with many descendants in later languages. But even with languages whose common etymological origin is much older, like English and Hungarian—or English and Chinese— and whose resemblance in sound is quite lost, that root can still be found. It takes a very deep reading of the original to zero in—through context, imagery, and above all meter, rhyme, form, and cadence—on the experience and urge that invaded the foreign poet.

So the second requirement for translation is a perfect or near-perfect reader. In our partnership, Turner claims that Ozsváth is very close to the perfect reader in this sense (and Ozsváth modestly denies it). The perfect reader is the one who can dig down into the original and unearth, in the form of a sort of parable, the real meaning of the word or phrase that the original poet used to translate the ur-experience, the poet's "fore-conceit," then communicate it in enough graphic force to the target-language partner. One could argue that the ideal reader of the source text and the ideal renderer of the final translated text should be the same person—Robert Fitzgerald's *Odyssey* and Schlegel's Shakespeare spring to mind—and many of the greatest translations have been the result of such a lucky accident. But we believe that a true partnership can be just as effective, and may even in some ways be superior. How?

When translating, we often remark that neither of us really understands a text until we try to translate it. That is, we must recapitulate to some degree the poet's own struggle to translate the poem from its original ur-language form. But familiarity can breed, if not contempt, a certain au fait or blasé superficiality of vision. We both teach literature. Was Turner, teaching Shakespeare, failing to get at the poet's deepest meanings because he was too familiar with the language and, hypnotized by its formal beauty and its common usage, took it at face value rather than recognizing its profound and significant oddity? Was Ozsváth doing the same with the great works of German and Hungarian literature that she taught? Partnership rubs our noses in the deep oddity, and can lead to that gash gold explosion of meaning out of misunderstanding. Perhaps the best reader and the best poet for a text should themselves have enough difference of perspective to recognize anomaly, to juxtapose, and to be forced into the sudden three-dimensional resolution of two different two-dimensional pictures. That resolution, to mix the metaphor, is the emergence of the ur-meaning from its long hibernation underground. Mixed metaphors and paradoxical parables are the currency of this work, this negotiation toward the hidden goal. Incidentally, this conclusion might well have a bearing on the nature of friendship.

This requirement for a perfect reader breaks another postmodern credo: that meaning is "always already" volatile, fugitive, and relative—or rather, is *only* volatile, fugitive, and relative. To the contrary, our contention is that there is a meaning to be found, and it is the right meaning. Of course the meaning may be enormously complex, rich, dynamic, and unpredictable like a living being, and expressible in many ways, but it is not a mere construction based on imbalances in power between the regimes of the two languages. Nor is the work of criticism what makes the meaning of the poem. The poet does not give us a bucket containing all the water and chemicals for making a cat or a cabbage or a rose. The poet gives us a live cat, cabbage, or rose. But it is the first cat, cabbage, or rose that ever was, and hard at first to fit into our world that never contained one before.

The third requirement for true translation is a relentless and learned pursuit of metaphor. When poets point to something in the world we share, like the moon or the hand or the river or the tree and, coupling it with some other shared experience not normally associated with it, uses it to adumbrate their meaning, something very important has taken place. The known thing is tweaked in some way that opens up a new field of meaning. The Ndembu people of Zambia, whom Turner knew as a child, had a word for this new-world-opening kind of symbol: *chijikijilu*. A chijikijilu is literally a blaze or waymark that a hunter, explorer, or traveler cuts on a tree to be able to safely enter new territory without getting lost, and to find the way back. It is a pathbreaker, it blazes a trail, it traces a track that we can retrace. Good translation requires a sort of worrying at the poet's metaphor, like the worrying of a dog with a bone, a gnawing and licking, a visceral response. The known half of the metaphor leads back to the safety of known territory, where, as Wittgenstein says, "whereof we cannot speak, thereof we must remain silent." The unknown half of the metaphor points to and creates logogenesis and functional neology. If, as Wittgenstein also says, the limits of my language are the limits of my world, then the world itself is enlarged when the language itself is thus bootstrapped into new expressiveness.

As translators, we would sometimes spend an hour or more worrying at one metaphor in the original. As we did so we realized that it lit up a whole poem or a whole block of text; little double entendres nearby emerged, the metaphor became part of an elaborate conceit worked through by the poet in the first place. The good common reader often will not consciously spot such patterns and connections, but they help generate that magic and memorability that draws us back to those particular metaphorical details in moments of stress or joy when we need poetry to state our minds. And those metaphors are the great resource of the translator in catching the atmosphere and thrust of the original. Poor translators, when they come across an odd use of a detail in the original, will often substitute a generic term or abstract enabler of a smooth sentence, and so lose the specificity of the metaphor and its visceral potential.

The fourth requirement for real translation is music: the music, in this case, of meter, rhyme, form, and prosody in general. In the hazardous journey toward the ur-language heart of a poem in another language, and, in the even more vertiginous journey back to the light of a different natural language, it is very easy to go astray. Meter, especially, has been the Virgil or Beatrice that leads us through the underworld of a poem's meaning and prevents us from getting lost. Here some important distinctions need to be made, and perhaps a paradox will help.

It is easier to translate metered poetry than free verse.

By "translate" here we mean *really* translate, that is, translate into the same verse form as the original, with the same structure of feet and stress and rhyme scheme and stanza form. Of course, to do so is technically very difficult, but this is part of the job of a competent poet anyway. To translate metered verse into free verse may well do more harm than good: the poem is then literally lost in translation, since what makes a poem a poem is largely the tone and cadence and music of it, the poet's voice, attitude, mood and sly collusion with the reader.

A good listener who has heard people speaking in many languages can often learn a great deal about the meaning of an overheard conversation in an unknown language simply from its prosody, which is largely shared across cultures and is part of our shared human inheritance. We know when a question is being asked, when the partners are lovers, when somebody is being told to do something, when it is a secret, when someone is making fun or expressing scorn or sharing reminiscences or upbraiding or apologizing or comforting or lying. Even dogs have some of these abilities.

But poetry's medium of transmission, since we ceased to communicate poems chiefly by oral memory, is written words. How are we to get the cues we got from our overheard conversation? The point of meter and form is that it provides a firm and predictable framework against which such prosodic variations and departures can be detected.

Here even more explanation is required. In these days when only pop song writers and well-educated literary scholars understand meter, it needs to be pointed out that meter is not a sing-song repetition but a basic beat against which all kinds of variations, expressing intent, emphasis, and feeling stand out. Take the first line of Shakespeare's Sonnet 18:

Shall I compare thee to a summer's day

Nobody literate would recite the line according to the basic beat, da DUM, da DUM, da DUM, da DUM, da DUM:

Shall **I** com**pare** thee **to** a **sum**mer's **day**

The basic beat is understood, but now the line can take several forms, each with its own emotional implication:

Shall I com**pare** thee to a **sum**mer's **day**

(In despair of finding the right metaphor for you, let's try a summer's day.)

Shall **I** compare **thee** to a summer's day

(What right have I, poor poet, to compare glorious you to anything?)

Shall **I** compare thee to a summer's day

(Another poet has compared you to a summer's day: now it's my turn.)

Shall I compare thee to a summer's day

(If I were to compare you to a summer's day, . . .)

Or even

Shall I compare **thee** to a summer's day

(Poets have compared lots of people to a summer's day: let's try it on you.)

Little shifts within the firm stave of the meter could suggest all kinds of other aspects of this hugely complex relationship.

And this is why free verse is harder to translate for a competent poet than metered verse. Meter (assisted by rhyme, alliteration, etc.) preserves in its implied tension between the logic and grammar on one hand and the musical beat on the other the original voice of the poet. Without meter, the only guides the translator has are logic, grammar, and the dictionary, or a gifted native speaker who has learned the poem orally from the poet's own tradition. And so we're back to prosody again, because all human cultures have a stock of metered poetry against which the characteristic sound of free verse can be gauged.

As we put it in our introduction to the Radnóti collection:

> . . . the cadence of poetry is already prior to and in common between all languages. One of the unnoticed peculiarities of the Orpheus myth is that though Orpheus is described as a poet rather than as a musician, it is the sweetness of his song, of his

lyre, of his music that persuades the masters of the Underworld to release Eurydice. We think the problem can be resolved by interpreting music in the myth as poetic meter: Minos and Rhadamanthus might not understand the surface language of a particular national lexicon and syntax, but recognize, as the root recognizes the sap, the ur-language of measure and cadence. So if the translator has faith in the ur-language—one might almost say, if he does not once look behind to check whether the "literal" sense is following—he may yet lead the redeemed meaning up into the light. In other words, since English is descended from the same deep root as Magyar, any music of which Magyar is capable exists also in English. To recover it is like, as Michelangelo put it, cutting away the stone to reveal the statue; the statue is waiting in the stone, if one has faith that it is.[5]

Goethe recognizes the green-gold tree of life as the same tree as that of language, whose buds and flowers are poems. But how to get from one branch to another? Our translation method may be likened to that of a tree-climber who, unable to reach another branch without falling, works his way back to the crotch where the two branches divide to discover their common source, then retraces the growth path of the other branch to find the same flower there. In Rilke's first sonnet to Orpheus (surely echoing Goethe's "golden tree"), he symbolizes the voice of the first poet, Orpheus, as a growing tree:

A tree ascending there. O pure transcension!
O Orpheus sings! O tall tree in the ear!

At the end of the poem he addresses Orpheus directly:

you built them temples in their sense of sound.[6]

For Rilke, as for Goethe, poetry is the further flowering of the evolutionary process that built the world and builds it still. The image has an older lineage too: the communion of humans is likened by the Hebrew poet to the vine and the branches, and the kingdom of heaven is likened to a mustard seed that grows into a tree where birds come and nest in the branches. The world tree—Yggdrasil, Jianmu, Iroko, Ashvattha, Yax Imix Che—is a pancultural archetype. But the branching of that growth can sometimes persuade us that our fellow branches are alien to us. Translation is the act that claims the unity of the whole tree and insists that the same sap flows through all the branches. Verse translation is the art of building a temple of sound—of meter and rhyme—that reproduces in the terms of one branch the flower of another.

ENDNOTES

1. Johann Wolfgang von Goethe, *The Project Gutenberg EBook of Faust, Part I,* "Studierzimmer," 124. http://www.gutenberg.org/cache/epub/2229/pg2229.html

2. Johann Peter Eckermann, *Gespräche mit Goethe in den letzten Jahren seines Lebens* (Munich: Beck, 1984), 198.

3. *Foamy Sky: The Major Poems of Miklós Radnóti*, trans. and ed, Zsuzsanna Ozsvath and Frederick Turner (Princeton: Princeton University Press, 1992), xli–xlii.

4. In this sense, the Foucauldian picture of irreconcilable cultural perspectives and the Feyerabendian picture of science as a purely political act are a strange humanist revival of the creationist view of a separate creation that Camper maintained.

5. Ozsvath and Turner, xliv.

6. Rainer Maria Rilke, *Poems*, trans. J.B. Leishman and Stephen Spender (New York: Alfred Knopf, 1996), 129. This masterly translation is the product of another partnership.

List of English and German Titles

Epigraph for an Introduction to *The West-East Divan*	"Wer das Dichten will verstehen," in *Epen, West-Ostlicher Divan, Theatergtedichte*, 3
The Luck of Love, 1769-70	Das Glück der Liebe, 1769-70
Dedication, 1770	Zueignung, 1770
Maying, 1771	Mailied, 1771
Welcome and Farewell, 1771	Willkommen und Abschied, 1771
Wild Rose, 1771	Heidenröslein, 1771
The New Amadis, 1771–1774	Der neue Amadis, 1771–1774
Wanderer's Storm Song, 1772	Wanderers Sturmlied, 1772
Mahomet's Song, 1772–1773	Mahomets Gesang, 1772–1773
Prometheus, 1773	Prometheus, 1773
Ganymede, 1774	Ganymed, 1774
The King in Thule, 1774	Der König in Thule, 1774
To Cousin Kronos, the Coachman, 1774	An Schwager Kronos, 1774
On the Lake, 1775	Auf dem See, 1775
The Artist's Evening Song, 1775	Künstlers Abendlied, 1775
The Bliss of Grief, 1775	Wonne der Wehmut, 1775
Wanderer's Night Song (1), 1776	Wanderers Nachtlied (1), 1776
To Charlotte von Stein, 1776	An Charlotte von Stein, 1776
Restless Love, 1776	Rastlose Liebe, 1776
Winter Journey in the Harz, 1777	Harzreise im Winter, 1777
To the Moon, 1777	An den Mond, 1777
All Things the Gods Bestow, 1777	Alles gaben die Goetter, 1777
Take This to Heart, 1777	Beherzigung, 1777
The Fisherman, 1778	Der Fischermann, 1778
Song of the Spirits upon the Waters, 1779	Gesang der Geister über den Wassern, 1779
Song of the Parcae, 1779	"Das Lied der Parzen" (*Iphigenie auf Tauris, Die Weimarer Dramen*) 1779
Wanderer's Night Song (2), 1780	Wanderers Nachtlied (2), 1780
Night Thoughts, 1781	Nachtgedanken, 1781

Human Limitations, 1781	Grenzen der Menschheit, 1781
My Goddess, 1781	Meine Gottin, 1781
The Elf-King, 1782	Erlkönig, 1782
Divinity, early 1780s	Das Göttliche, early 1780s
"Joyful and Woeful ...", 1788	Egmont, 1788
Morning Complaints, 1788	Morgenklagen, 1788
Five Roman Elegies (1788–1790):	Fünf Römische Elegien (1788–1790):
I. Speak, O stones of Rome ...	I. Saget Steine mir an ...
III. Do not regret, beloved, ...	III. Lass dich Geliebte, nicht reun ...
V. Happy I find myself ...	V. Froh empfind ich mich ...
VII. How merry I am in Rome! ...	VII. O wie fuehl ich ich in Rom mich so froh ...
IX. Flames, autumnal, glow ...	IX. Herbstlich leuchtet die Flamme ...
The Nearness of the Beloved, 1795	Nähe der Geliebten, 1795
The Silent Sea, 1796	Meeres Stille, 1796

Three Poems from *Wilhelm Meisters Lehrjahre* (1795–96):

"D'you know that land where lemon blossoms ..."	"Kennst du das Land wo die Zitronen blühn ...
"Ah, none but those who yearn ..."	"Nur wer die Sehnsucht kennt ..."
"Who never ate his bread with tears ..."	"Wer nie sein Brot mit Tränen ass ..."
The Sorcerer's Apprentice, 1797	Der Zauberlehrling, 1797
The God and the Dancer, 1797	Der Gott und die Bajadere, 1797
The Bride of Corinth, 1797	Die Braut von Korinth, 1797
The Metamorphosis of the Plants, 1799	Die Metamorphose der Pflanzen, 1799
World Soul, 1801	Weltseele, 1801
Nature and Art, 1802	Natur und Kunst, 1802
Permanence in Change, 1803	Dauer im Wechsel, 1803
Night Song, 1804	Nachtgesang, 1804
The Sonnet, 1806	Das Sonett, 1806
The Metamorphosis of the Animals, 1806	Die Metamorphose der Tiere, 1806
Farewell, 1807	Abschied, 1807
The Lover Writes Again, 1807–8	Die Liebende abermals, 1807–8
8 Poems from *The West-East Divan*:	8 Gedichte aus *Der West-Ostliche Divan* in *Epen, West-Ostlicher Divan, Theaterge-dichte*:

185

Johann Wolfgang von Goethe (1749–1832) is the most prominent and influential figure in German letters. Born in Frankfurt, he published his breakout novel, *The Sorrows of Young Werther*, in 1774 at the age of twenty-five, and the first part of his lyric masterpiece, *Faust*, in 1808. Goethe was a poet, novelist, literary critic, diplomat, and scientist, publishing works across the spectrum, from tales of romantic despair to dense scientific tomes. His involvement in the literary movement *Sturm und Drang* was formative in the development of Romanticism, and his writings created a new paradigm in German high culture.

Dr. Zsuzsanna Ozsváth is the Leah and Paul Lewis Chair in Holocaust Studies and Professor of Literature and the History of Ideas in the School of Arts and Humanities at the University of Texas at Dallas. Her work focuses on two areas: Holocaust literature and poetry translation. She has published a number of articles, dealing with aesthetic and ethical issues in French, German, and Hungarian literature as well as with the relationship between art and totalitarian ideology. Her chilling memoir, *When the Danube Ran Red* (Syracuse University Press) tells the story of her childhood in Hungary, living under the threat of the Holocaust. .

Frederick Turner, the Founders Professor of Arts and Humanities at the University of Texas at Dallas, is an award-winning poet, cultural critic, playwright, philosopher of science, interdisciplinary scholar, aesthetician, essayist, and translator. He is the author of twenty-eight books, a fellow of the Texas Institute of Letters, and the recipient of the prestigious Levinson Prize for poetry. Turner earned his undergraduate and graduate degrees from Oxford University. He is also a second-degree black belt in karate.

Together, Ozsváth and Turner co-translated *Foamy Sky: The Major Poems of Miklós Radnóti* (Princeton University Press), Attila József's *The Iron-Blue Vault: Selected Poems* (Bloodaxe), and *Light Among the Shade: Eight–Hundred–Years of Hungarian Poetry* (Syracuse University Press). Their co-translations have been awarded the Milán Füst Prize, the highest literary prize in Hungary, and the publishing prize of the Hungarian Ministry of Culture and Education at the Frankfurt Book Fair.

PARTNERS

ALLRED
CAPITAL MANAGEMENT

RAYMOND JAMES®

SUBSCRIBERS

THANK YOU ALL FOR YOUR SUPPORT.
WE DO THIS FOR YOU,
AND COULD NOT DO IT WITHOUT YOU.

MICHÈLE AUDIN · *One Hundred Twenty-One Days*
translated by Christiana Hills · FRANCE

BAE SUAH · *Recitation*
translated by Deborah Smith · SOUTH KOREA

EDUARDO BERTI · *The Imagined Land*
translated by Charlotte Coombe · ARGENTINA

CARMEN BOULLOSA · *Texas: The Great Theft* · *Before* · *Heavens on Earth*
translated by Samantha Schnee · Peter Bush · Shelby Vincent · MEXICO

Cleave, Sarah, ed. · *Banthology: Stories from Banned Nations* · IRAN, IRAQ, LIBYA,
SOMALIA, SUDAN, SYRIA & YEMEN

LEILA S. CHUDORI · *Home*
translated by John H. McGlynn · INDONESIA

ANANDA DEVI · *Eve Out of Her Ruins*
translated by Jeffrey Zuckerman · MAURITIUS

ALISA GANIEVA · *Bride and Groom* · *The Mountain and the Wall*
translated by Carol Apollonio · RUSSIA

ANNE GARRÉTA · *Sphinx* · *Not One Day*
translated by Emma Ramadan · FRANCE

JÓN GNARR · *The Indian* · *The Pirate* · *The Outlaw*
translated by Lytton Smith · ICELAND

NOEMI JAFFE · *What are the Blind Men Dreaming?*
translated by Julia Sanches & Ellen Elias-Bursac · BRAZIL

CLAUDIA SALAZAR JIMÉNEZ · *Blood of the Dawn*
translated by Elizabeth Bryer · PERU

JUNG YOUNG MOON · *Vaseline Buddha*
translated by Yewon Jung · SOUTH KOREA

JOSEFINE KLOUGART · *Of Darkness*
translated by Martin Aitken · DENMARK

YANICK LAHENS · *Moonbath*
translated by Emily Gogolak · HAITI

ÓFEIGUR SIGURÐSSON · *Öræfi: The Wasteland*
translated by Lytton Smith · ICELAND

SERHIY ZHADAN · *Voroshilovgrad*
translated by Reilly Costigan-Humes & Isaac Stackhouse Wheeler · UKRAINE

FORTHCOMING FROM DEEP VELLUM

GOETHE · *The Golden Goblet: Selected Poems*
translated by Zsuzsanna Ozsváth and Frederick Turner · GERMANY

JUNG YOUNG MOON · *Seven Samurai Swept Away in a River*
translated by Yewon Jung · SOUTH KOREA

DMITRY LIPSKEROV · *The Tool and the Butterflies*
translated by Reilly Costigan-Humes & Isaac Stackhouse Wheeler · RUSSIA

DOROTA MASŁOWSKA · *Honey, I Killed the Cats*
translated by Benjamin Paloff · POLAND

JESSICA SCHIEFAUER · *Girls Lost*
translated by Saskia Vogel · SWEDEN

KIM YIDEUM · *Blood Sisters*
translated by Ji yoon Lee · SOUTH KOREA

MATHILDE CLARK · *Lone Star*
translated from the Danish by Martin Aitken · DENMARK

ANNE GARRÉTA · *Dans l'beton*
translated from the French by Emma Ramadan · FRANCE

MÄRTA TIKKANEN · *The Love Story of the Century*
translated from Swedish by Stina Katchadourian · FINLAND

CPSIA information can be obtained
at www.ICGtesting.com
Printed in the USA
LVHW111538150519
617949LV00003B/563/P